GUIDELINES

VOL 33 / PART 1
January–April 2017

Commissioned by **David Spriggs***; Edited by* **Lisa Cherrett**

GW00691609

Guidelines © BRF 2017

The Bible Reading Fellowship
15 The Chambers, Vineyard, Abingdon OX14 3FE
brf.org.uk; biblereadingnotes.org.uk

ISBN 978 0 85746 440 8

Distributed in Australia by Mediacom Education Inc., PO Box 610, Unley, SA 5061.
Tel: 1800 811 311; Fax: 08 8297 8719;
E-mail: admin@mediacom.org.au
Available also from all good Christian bookshops in Australia.
For individual and group subscriptions in Australia:
Mrs Rosemary Morrall, PO Box W35, Wanniassa, ACT 2903.

Distributed in New Zealand by Scripture Union Wholesale, PO Box 760, Wellington
Tel: 04 385 0421; Fax: 04 384 3990; E-mail: suwholesale@clear.net.nz

Publications distributed to more than 60 countries

Acknowledgments

Printed by Gutenberg Press, Tarxien, Malta.

Suggestions for using *Guidelines*

Set aside a regular time and place, if possible, when you can read and pray undisturbed. Before you begin, take time to be still and, if you find it helpful, use the BRF prayer.

In *Guidelines*, the introductory section provides context for the passages or themes to be studied, while the units of comment can be used daily, weekly, or whatever best fits your timetable. You will need a Bible (more than one if you want to compare different translations) as Bible passages are not included. At the end of each week is a 'Guidelines' section, offering further thoughts about, or practical application of what you have been studying.

Occasionally, you may read something in *Guidelines* that you find particularly challenging, even uncomfortable. This is inevitable in a series of notes which draws on a wide spectrum of contributors, and doesn't believe in ducking difficult issues. Indeed, we believe that *Guidelines* readers much prefer thought-provoking material to a bland diet that only confirms what they already think.

If you do disagree with a contributor, you may find it helpful to go through these three steps. First, think about why you feel uncomfortable. Perhaps this is an idea that is new to you, or you are not happy at the way something has been expressed. Or there may be something more substantial—you may feel that the writer is guilty of sweeping generalisation, factual error, theological or ethical misjudgment. Second, pray that God would use this disagreement to teach you more about his word and about yourself. Third, think about what you will do as a result of the disagreement. You might resolve to find out more about the issue, or write to the contributor or the editors of *Guidelines*.

To send feedback, you may email or write to BRF at the addresses shown opposite. If you would like your comment to be included on our website, please email connect@brf.org.uk. You can also Tweet to @brfonline, using the hashtag #brfconnect.

Writers in this issue

Graham Usher is the Bishop of Dudley. An ecologist by background, he worked for 18 years in parish ministry in the north-east of England. He is one of the Church of England's environmental bishops and is the author of *Places of Enchantment: Meeting God in Landscapes* (SPCK, 2012).

Oldi Morava is currently working with Bible Society to translate the Old Testament into Albanian as part of an interconfessional team. He graduated from Redcliffe College with a BA in Applied Theology and later completed a Masters in Biblical Hebrew at Oxford University. He is married with one daughter.

Nigel G. Wright was Principal of Spurgeon's College from 2000 to 2013 and is a former President of the Baptist Union of Great Britain. He has written *Jesus Christ—the Alpha and the Omega* for BRF (2010).

Heather Fenton is the editor of *The Reader* and the Church in Wales *Highlights*, and was, at one time, editor of BRF's *Quiet Spaces*. She is a priest in the Church in Wales, where she serves as a Diocesan Rural Life Adviser.

David Fleming studied for the Baptist ministry in Oxford, specialising in Old Testament studies. Ordained in 1995, he has ministered in churches in Kent and Oxfordshire and is now the minister of Limbury Baptist Church in Luton.

C.L. Crouch is Associate Professor in Hebrew Bible at the University of Nottingham, where she teaches on the history of Israel and Judah, prophecy and the prophetic books, and ethics in and of the Hebrew Bible. She has written on the ethics of warfare, on biblical creation narratives, on the book of Deuteronomy and on Israelite ethnic identity.

Jeremy Duff is Principal of St Padarn's Institute, a new centre for ministry training in Wales. His book *The Elements of New Testament Greek* (2005) is Cambridge University Press's bestselling religion title. He has also written *Peter's Preaching* for BRF (2015).

David Kerrigan first joined BMS in 1983 and served in countries including Bangladesh and Sri Lanka, interspersed with periods of study and church leadership in the UK. He has been General Director of BMS World Mission since 2009.

The Editor writes...

A new year is a liminal moment for many people. Of course, on the threshold of the future, we are also prone to look back. Given this tendency, Deuteronomy is a helpful text. It presents us with God's people poised to enter the promised land, with Moses reminding them of the past as well as making provision for their life ahead. At its heart is the foundational truth: 'The Lord is our God, the Lord alone. You shall love the Lord your God' (6:4–5). Oldi Morava brings all his insights as a Bible Society translator to engage our hearts and minds with this God.

First, though, Bishop Graham Usher helps us engage with God through various landscapes as he intriguingly explores the ways in which they provide a context and medium for God's self-revelation.

Next comes the first of three studies of Matthew 15—28 through the year. Our guide is Nigel Wright, who has written many books and served as Principal in a theological training college. He introduces his notes by saying, 'Jesus was not, and is not, predictable'.

Heather Fenton links the themes of journey and landscape as she shares some insights about three Celtic saints and the way they were helped by the Psalms. Patrick, David and Columba are her guides.

We then return to the Old Testament. David Fleming takes us into the promised land, courtesy of the book of Joshua, reminding us that God's people are rarely settled. As they travel, they need to renew their covenant with God, and even in their land there are challenges and temptations on all sides.

Carly Crouch, a young American scholar, illuminates Micah, one of the 'minor prophets', who speaks to both Jerusalem and Samaria. The second half of the book includes Micah 6:8, a famous verse that 'lays out in memorable phrasing the foundation of the good life'. Here we find historical insights and spiritual challenge.

Finally we turn to the cross and resurrection. Jeremy Duff takes us through John 18—20, showing us Jesus' death against the double background of the Jewish leaders' duplicity and God's unfolding purpose of redemption. At last the glory of the resurrection bursts through, with the unforgettable cameos of Jesus meeting first Mary Magdalene and then the other disciples. Finally, David Kerrigan helps us understand the missional implications of these events. As with the new year, so with crucifixion and resurrection we stand on the threshold of new beginnings.

David Spriggs

The BRF Prayer

Almighty God,
you have taught us that your word is a lamp for our
feet and a light for our path. Help us, and all who
prayerfully read your word, to deepen our
fellowship with you and with each other through your love.
And in so doing may we come to know you more fully,
love you more truly, and follow more faithfully in
the steps of your son Jesus Christ, who lives and
reigns with you and the Holy Spirit,
one God for evermore. Amen.

Divine landscapes

Do you feel close to God in the great outdoors? It seems that, for many people, God is particularly close to them as they walk through their local park, look up into the canopy of trees, climb a hill or walk along a shingle beach with the sea rattling its breath in and out. Life seems to slow down, time has a different quality, and the still small voice of calm seems close. We might find ourselves drawn into the prayer of silence, or we might yearn to let out a loud cry of praise for all of creation, joining with the psalmist's delight: 'Let everything that breathes praise the Lord' (Psalm 150:6).

When we turn the pages of scripture we continually discover God making himself known in landscapes. As his people cross deserts, sit by riversides, wait in gardens or encounter God speaking from a burning bush or passing by the cleft of the mountains, so God is made known to them.

The inbreaking of God's presence as he makes his glory known is described as a theophany. By reflecting on biblical texts, we discover how God is continuing to make himself known to us in and through his creation, for 'ever since the creation of the world [God's] eternal power and divine nature, invisible though they are, have been understood and seen through the things he has made' (Romans 1:20).

We learn more about the Creator as we pause in a landscape and take it all in, discovering afresh the goodness, wisdom and almighty power of God shining forth. Nature is God's gift to us, and the closer we get in touch with it, being present within it, the more we experience God's revelation to us through the focus of our gaze.

Biblical quotations are taken from the New Revised Standard Version.

2–8 January

1 The trees of the field shall clap their hands

Isaiah 55:6–13

The prophet Isaiah keeps writing beautiful poetic language to encourage his people. The trauma of the Babylonian exile had left deep scars, and the people of Judah, having seen their capital city destroyed and families torn apart, were questioning their belief in the God of their ancestors. The prophet uses this poem to inspire his people once again to dream the seemingly impossible.

This passage is a beautiful and exuberant finale to the whole of Deutero-Isaiah (chapters 40—55). It speaks of a God who is faithful and life-giving. To a people living in arid conditions, 'the rain and the snow' (v. 10) would have prompted thoughts of the soil being prepared so that crops could flourish and bring an ample harvest. It is a metaphor for God's word, which transforms and brings abundant life.

This is such good news that it leads to great rejoicing. Again, Isaiah speaks in rich metaphors of the seemingly impossible. Mountains burst into song and the trees give accompaniment as they clap their hands (v. 12). The picture of singing trees is not limited to Isaiah, as we find the metaphor also in other passages, such as 1 Chronicles 16:33 and Psalm 96:12–13. We can note that in each of these passages there is a connection between singing trees and God's judgement. Throughout the book of Isaiah, thorn trees and briers (v. 13) have been seen as a symbol of judgement (5:6; 7:23–25; 32:13). Now, these plants are suppressed and, in their place, cypress trees and myrtle flourish. Places of abandonment and desolation become fertile again, just as there is a new life awaiting the exiles after their Babylonian experience.

The invasion of the land by an empire that destroyed everything in its way would have left its effect also on the natural environment, just as wars today leave an often-forgotten legacy of pollution and destruction. The promise of God's restoration, with the hope of healing and peace, is good news not only for humans but also for the ecosystem.

We live in a world where there is much destruction of the natural environment. Forests are disappearing at an alarming rate, affecting soil, rivers, species diversity, climate and much else. We too can speak of the trees groaning under this destruction. The question for us is 'How can we bring healing and restoration so that the trees might sing and clap their hands?'

2 A voice from a burning bush

Exodus 3:1–17

John Muir (1838–1914) founded many of the famous national parks, such as Yosemite, in the United States. He was a great conservationist who, as he listened to the sound of the wind in tree canopies, spoke of their range of 'voices', each species of tree singing its own song as it moved.

The burning bush sings another song. From the fire that does not consume it comes God's voice. The voice fills Moses with such awe and wonder that he hides his face, afraid to look on God's presence (v. 6). He thinks of every excuse not to undertake the task required of him, questioning himself and his God (vv. 11, 13). God also seems reluctant to disclose himself, hiding in the fiery bush and in the confusing self-description, 'I am who I am' (v. 14). Yet this holy conversation equips Moses for his task, to go to Pharaoh, to bring his people out of Egypt, and to lead them towards a land flowing with milk and honey.

The conversation is marked by holy ground, where shoes are removed (v. 5). If you visit a Muslim mosque, Hindu temple, or Sikh gurdwara, you are similarly asked to take off your shoes. In the natural world, too, there are places where you feel that you are treading on holy ground, places where God seems close. Our forebears took the idea of sacred forests into the construction of the great medieval cathedrals: the columns in the nave represent the towering trunks of mighty trees, while the fan vaulting overhead is a representation in stone of the branches of the tree canopy. The vaulting is decorated with foliage and, high in the roof, wooden bosses of 'green men', their faces surrounded with leaves, tongues often stuck out as if they are spewing their hedgerow meal.

Research has found that spending time in woods and forests can slow the pulse rate, leading to a greater awareness of silence and tranquillity as we enter a different rhythm of life. It has been shown that people in hospital get better more quickly if they can look out at trees, and prisoners with a view of trees from their cell are less likely to reoffend than those with no view of greenery. Perhaps this was why St Bernard of Clairvaux (1090–1153) commented, 'Believe me, you will find more lessons in the woods than in books.'

3 Up out of the water

The River Jordan, which has its source on Mount Hermon and flows south, taking in the Sea of Galilee and then flowing a further 65 miles to the Dead Sea, is a significant landmark. Moses came within sight of this river, and it was eventually crossed by Joshua as he led the Israelites into the promised land. Crossing this water meant the fulfilment of God's promise and the final end to slavery and desert wandering.

These themes are present as John the Baptist calls the crowds to a new repentance and a new passing through the waters, urging them to set their faces in a new direction. So, in a landscape that is pregnant with meaning, Jesus enters the scene and is baptised by his cousin John. Like the previous generations, these people of Israel are in a kind of slavery, under Roman occupation. It is also a time when the leaders of the day are being found wanting, even with their strict moral codes. This is the time when Jesus slips into the water to embrace his people's history.

The symbol of the Spirit above the water (v. 10) takes us back to the creation narrative (Genesis 1:2), reminding us that this is also a new creation story. The symbol of the dove brings echoes of Noah's story, with the dove that was sent out of the ark and did not return (Genesis 8:12). Now the bird makes its reappearance, reminding us that this story is also about the renewal of God's covenant promise. The voice that speaks of 'the Beloved' (v. 11) takes us back to the story of Abraham and his beloved son, Isaac (Genesis 22:2). Now another story of trust and faithfulness is being played out.

In our baptism we are given a new creation; Gods sets his seal upon our heart and leads us on a journey of trust and faithfulness. We, too, slip into the river of Jesus' life and passion, death and resurrection. Many of us are reminded of this during the Easter liturgy. As the fire of the resurrection is brought in and lights the church, we proclaim, 'He is risen indeed, Alleluia!' and we renew our baptismal vows. The river flows through us again so that we might be more alive with Jesus. We plunge into a new way of being, living and acting in the world, so that we might become a blessing to others.

4 Stirred-up water

Britain is dotted with holy wells. In Derbyshire there is a tradition of dressing wells with flowers during festivals, and many communities treasure stories of healing received, forgiveness offered and accepted, and reconciliation encountered at the local holy well. The healing reputation of wells resonates with the story of the man who has been waiting for years by the pool of Bethsaida.

Jesus, on entering Jerusalem (v. 1), goes first not to the powerful and intellectual, but to the outcasts of his day—those whom others are ashamed of, whom they want to ignore and block from their minds. These people are gathered at a huge pool of therapeutic waters, which archaeologists now believe to have been a pagan site of healing. The local tradition said that when there was a surge in the spring and the waters were stirred up, the first person to dive in would be cured. The particular man whom Jesus approaches speaks out a lament of loneliness because he has no one to lift him into the water.

Jean Vanier, founder of L'Arche, who has worked for decades to bring wholeness to people with disabilities by providing communities of care and love, wrote, 'It is as if Jesus cannot contain himself; he loves this man as he is, just as he loved the Samaritan woman. He yearns to liberate him from all the powers of despair within him, that he be fully alive' (Vanier, *Drawn Into the Mystery of Jesus through the Gospel of John*, DLT, 2004, p. 105).

The most moving Confirmation service that I've taken was one where a man with profound disabilities, when asked whether he wanted to be confirmed, replied, 'I love Jesus.' He went on saying the same words ever louder throughout the service. His sincerity and passion moved many of us to tears, especially when he enjoyed splashing the water around in the baptismal font.

Sitting by a well, watching the water bubbling out, reminds us of the refreshment that God's love offers us. If you put your hand against the opening, its force pushes against you; you simply can't stop the water from gushing out. Likewise, God's love is always offering, always providing more, always spreading out. You can't stop it.

5 The cleft of a rock

Exodus 33:18—34:8

Mountains in the Bible are often places of theophany. On Mount Sinai, Moses, having asked to see God's face, glimpses the back of God's grandeur from his hiding place in the cleft of the rock. Some commentators suggest that to see God's 'back' (33:23) implies seeing the place 'where he just was'. The Welsh poet R.S. Thomas spoke of 'such a fast God, always before us and leaving as we arrive'. Moses was not able to see God, just the place where he had been.

In the mountains, God is met in emptiness within a barren landscape. All of our images of God are emptied and we find that we can't capture or package God. He is discovered in unexpected ways. It is on the mountain that we see Moses' authentication as the mediator between God and his people. God's presence is experienced in smoke, cloud, fire, the sound of trumpets and booming thunder.

Often we fail to see God's presence because we are not attentive enough to the sacrament of the present moment. It seems to be easier to see where God 'just was' when we look back on our day. The Ignatian practice of 'examen' is a way of reviewing the day prayerfully: usually at the end of the day, we recall the events that have involved us, the failures along the way and those moments of God's gracious giftedness. It's then that we notice where God has been.

The Christian pilgrimage involves persistence during those times when God hides his face from us. It is by feeling held in the cleft of the rock, as if in the palm of a hand, peering through the gaps between the fingers, that we find our way back to God. The mountaineer who is looking at a mountain in swirling mist sees a part here, and then it disappears, and another part is revealed over there. As we abide in God, so we build a picture and discover something of what it is to be in his presence.

A cleft can be formed when something is torn apart, broken and opened up. Life events might make us feel like that. Perhaps it is in those gaps, and those torn and broken places, that we discover God.

6 Led up a high mountain

Luke 9:28–36

If the experience of God on Mount Sinai was one of inaccessibility and transcendence, God is encountered on the mount of transfiguration with clarity and immanence. The experience is framed in Luke's Gospel in the context of prayer as the purpose for the mountain climb.

The Gospels tell us of previous journeys in the uplands. Mary travelled across the hill country of Judea to visit her relative Elizabeth, who was also expecting a child (Luke 1:39–40). Jesus frequently went into the lonely places of the hills around the Sea of Galilee for rest and prayer (Luke 6:12), and delivered his most famous sermon on a mountainside (Matthew 5—7). There, it was as if a new Moses was speaking. The gathered people heard it all in a silence reminiscent of Elijah's experience of God (1 Kings 19:12–13). Now, Moses and Elijah are drawn into a revelation on the top of a mountain, which is experienced by three of the disciples.

The Orthodox theologian Vigen Guroian notes, 'For a few precious moments Peter and James and John were also transformed by the light; they were filled with the presence of God and with spiritual eyes saw in Christ the glory of their own transfigured humanity' (Guroian, *Inheriting Paradise: Meditations on gardening*, Eerdmans, 1999, p. 51).

The story sets the direction of travel as we turn in the Gospel towards Jerusalem. Jesus is the new Moses (the new law-giver) and the new Elijah (the new prophet). Peter wants to box up the experience and hold on to it, but we discover through him that we can't keep hold of God. When we are in the mountains, we may want to hold on to our experience of God's presence, caught between silent awe and a desire to give the moment expression.

Mountain-top experiences never last for ever, though, and we are faced with the daily realities of life. As if to underline this fact, if we read on in Luke's Gospel we find a man bringing the disciples down to earth with the need for his son to be cured of something like epilepsy (9:37–43). By healing the boy, Jesus enables both father and child—the only son and only heir of the family—to be lifted up and receive the glory of the mountain-top.

Guidelines

Have you ever experienced God's presence amid nature? How did God manifest himself and what did the experience teach you about him?

Take a close look at something you pick up from the natural world. Examine its texture, colours, smell, the sound it makes and (only if you are sure it's edible) its taste. Praise God for all that you observe.

How can we live in a way that enables the trees of the field to flourish, and so join in the collective song of praise with all of creation?

The Victorian poet Elizabeth Barrett Browning (1806–61) wrote:

> *Earth's crammed with heaven,*
> *and every common bush afire with God;*
> *but only he who sees, takes off his shoes,*
> *the rest sit round it and pluck blackberries.*
>
> FROM *AURORA LEIGH*

Can you share any experience of 'every common bush afire with God' with others?

> Lord, you whom we glimpse
> in the cleft of a rock,
> from a mountain view,
> amid stirred waters,
> we praise you for your creation,
> and ask that you will inspire us daily
> to fill our hearts and minds with awe and praise
> in the presence of your wonder: Amen

1 The scouring desert

Genesis 16:1–9; 21:8–21

The writers of the scriptures are generally ill at ease in the desert. It is 'an arid wasteland with poisonous snakes and scorpions (Deuteronomy

8:15), 'a howling wilderness waste' (Deuteronomy 32:10) and a 'land ruined and laid waste' (Jeremiah 9:12). The desert is devoid of water and food, and affords no protection from the intense heat of the sun by day or the extreme cold of the starlit sky by night. It tests the wit of human survival.

Hagar had it hard. She lived within the household of Abraham and Sarah, where there had been no gift of an heir, despite God's promise that Abraham would be 'the ancestor of a multitude of nations' (Genesis 17:4). As a slave-girl, she probably had no choice but to accept being used as a surrogate mother, and little option but to run away when Sarah, her mistress, noticed her looking 'with contempt' on her (16:4–5).

It's in the wilderness, by a spring of water, that Hagar meets God. He asks her, 'Where have you come from and where are you going?' (16:8). She knows where she has come from, because she has run away from her mistress, but she has no answer to the second part of the question. She is confused in the desert place, fearful of what has been and of what the future holds, especially the immediate future in that hostile environment.

When Hagar is again cast out into the desert, this time with her young son (21:14), she finds a landscape in which her life is totally scoured—a place that is empty of all meaning. She has returned to her master's home once before, but can't return again. Giving up all hope, she places her dear son under a bush, knowing that, dehydrated, he will soon die. We can imagine the pitiful sight, so reminiscent of images in contemporary news reports, as she breaks down and weeps.

Again, God rescues her in that barren place. She is given what she needs as a well of water appears before her eyes (v. 19). So, while the desert is a fearsome place, it is also a place of encounter, renewal and hope, where God yearns that all might blossom. Isaiah describes it poetically, saying, 'The wilderness and the dry land shall be glad, the desert shall rejoice and blossom; like the crocus it shall blossom abundantly, and rejoice with joy and singing' (Isaiah 35:1–2a).

2 The desert of solitude

Luke 5:12–16

As we read the Gospels we often find Jesus leaving the daily busyness and demands of his ministry to be all alone with his Father (v. 16; see also Mark 1:35; 6:46; Luke 6:12) or to rest in the company of his disciples (Mark 6:31). These were nourishing and deeply lived times, which came after intense activity or when his mind was filled with questions and concerns. They were times for Jesus to be resourced by his Father so that he could go on doing everything he needed to do.

Similarly, many people find that they need time alone or in nature to rediscover themselves and to be recharged for all that they are doing. The value of these times for re-creation, and nature's role in recreating us into the people God would have us be, shouldn't be underestimated.

Having just healed a leprous man, Jesus' fame as a miracle worker and healer was spreading like wildfire through the marketplaces and fields of Galilee, attracting crowds of people. Luke says, 'But he would withdraw to deserted places and pray' (v. 16). In the Greek text, the imperfect tense is used, to show that this was not a one-off action; Jesus kept repeating it. Another way of translating the verse would be, 'But he continued to withdraw to deserted places and pray.'

When we see the word 'but', we know that there is a contrast between what lies before it and what comes after. Here, the word comes between crowds and deserted places, full and empty spaces. Jesus needed, and kept needing, to be on his own so that he could prioritise prayer. In a sense, he emptied himself in places that were full of people, and needed to be filled again in places that were empty of people but full of God.

It is important in this context to distinguish between solitude and loneliness. Jesus withdrew by himself in a contented way, so that the emptiness of the deserted places could be full of the presence of God. There, he was 100 per cent present to his Father, who became the totality of his gaze and attention.

Natural places continue to be arenas in which God can recreate us, as he did his Son, through his animating and wondrous presence.

3 The great and wide sea

Psalm 104:1–9, 24–31

John F. Kennedy remarked, 'It is an interesting biological fact that all of us have in our veins the exact same percentage of salt in our blood that exists in the ocean… And when we go back to the sea—whether it is to sail or to watch it—we are going back from whence we came.' Water covers 71 per cent of our planet's surface. About 96 per cent of that water is too salty to drink and would poison land for the growing of crops and rearing of cattle. Of the four per cent that is drinkable, a little under two per cent is in the form of ice.

Psalm 104 is a great hymn of praise, which we could imagine being sung accompanied by images from a TV natural history programme. The psalmist's camera lens swoops here and there, over mountains, up into the sky and through the branches of the trees. We know that the Pacific Ocean's Mariana Trench plumbs more than 35,000 feet (11,000 metres), and it's as if the psalmist takes us even into those depths. He writes of the many creatures that fill the oceans, with no suggestion that they are useful to humanity, only that they are bound up in God, enabling God himself to 'rejoice in his works' (v. 31).

The array of creatures from our seas often do look very alien to us. Take a tour of a fishmonger's counter, especially overseas, and you will find some mighty strange creatures from the deep. This incredible biodiversity, only a tiny fraction of which is thought to have been described so far, leads us to wonder at the 'creeping things innumerable… living things both small and great' (v. 25).

Yet we know too of their fragility and the way in which we are polluting the seas, overharvesting the fish and destroying the fine ecosystems of the ocean floor. In some parts of the oceans, depending on the pattern of the currents, there are vast floating rafts of plastic. Autopsies of dead sea birds and mammals often reveal intestines crammed full of plastic and nylon that has been discarded into the seas.

Psalm 104 reminds us that the seascape is God's as well. What might he be saying to us through the voice of tidal rhythms and the rattling of the shingle as the waves come up and down the beach?

4 So many fish

Luke 5:1–11

I once joined a group mackerel fishing off Whitby and realised that we must have been above a shoal: every time we let down our lines we immediately caught a dozen fish. It felt like a biblical catch. Soon we had to stop because we had far too many for supper. All our neighbours had gifts of fish that night.

The story of Jesus out fishing with his disciples is a beautiful one. Around the Sea of Galilee is a series of little bays that, from the point of view of someone in a boat, act like amphitheatres into which one can speak and be easily heard. Jesus was sitting in a boat, teaching, while the fishermen, who had caught nothing all night, washed their nets.

The very last thing these despondent and exhausted men, ready for their beds, would have wanted was to go out fishing again. The morning was not a good time for it. 'If you say so,' huffed the disciple Simon, like an awkward teenager (v. 5).

The disciples' experience was awe-inspiring as the nets were pulled in, full of fish, but it must also have been terrifying as the ropes began to snap and the weight of fish started to cause water to pour in over the side of the boat. No wonder Jesus speaks one of his most common sentences in the Gospels: 'Do not be afraid' (v. 10).

Here is a foretaste of the Christ who will gather up all things across the cosmos—earth and sea and sky—and unite them in God's purposes (Ephesians 1:10). No wonder it was terrifying!

The sea can terrify us and calm us in equal measure. Out on the sea, we can feel fragile and more alert to the elements and our reliance on human craft and skill. We use phrases such as 'all at sea' to describe a feeling of insecurity, and feel better when we know we have 'both feet on dry land'.

A walk along a stormy coast can blow the cobwebs away, drowning out the competing noises in our minds, and sea air makes us feel more alive and helps us to sleep better. On a calm day, the sound of gentle waves can soothe pains, angers and hurts. Their ebb and flow, when linked to our own prayers, can bring a new and healing rhythm to bewilderment and confusion.

5 Walking in the garden

Genesis 2:8–9; 3:1–8

The story of the garden of Eden lays out a stunning vision of the pre-Fall world that humans messed up. When they had disobeyed God by eating the forbidden fruit, Adam and Eve were deeply ashamed. We read that 'they heard the sound of the Lord God walking in the garden at the time of the evening breeze' (3:8) and hid themselves. We can imagine that every step God took echoed around them as if they were in cinema-quality Dolby surround sound.

The idea of God walking through the garden is, whilst anthropomorphic, a beautiful image. We connect with the earth as we walk on it, and the rhythm of walking allows us to lose ourselves in the flow of movement. Frédéric Gros, in his book *A Philosophy of Walking*, writes about walking as a way of 'experiencing the real'. In Genesis 3, it is as if God is fathoming out exactly what has happened in his gift of paradise, as he walks.

Jesus kept walking and kept inviting others to come and follow him so as to experience the real life he was offering them. The disciples moved at Jesus' pace, discovering what it was to walk the earth, feeling underfoot the hard ground, the ground where the birds pecked and the thistles grew, and the soft loam that produced a harvest of wheat. By walking at Jesus' pace, they began to hear the cry of the poor and sick, see the marginalised and ostracised, and respond to those in need of love and healing.

The theologian Dan Hardy (1930–2007) wrote that Jesus walked 'step by step through the land, and after every set of steps he met someone, stood by someone, one to one, and in some way he touched and healed each one' (*Wording a Radiance: Parting conversations on God and the church*, SCM, 2010).

This was Jesus' way. He keeps drawing us back to walk with God in his garden of delight at the time of the refreshing evening breeze. Perhaps you have a garden, or visit a garden, where you experience this for yourself? On the winding path of life, by the colourful herbaceous borders, and also amidst the debris around the compost bins and the scrappy parts of the garden, God is welcoming us home.

6 Gardens of sorrow and delight

John 19:38—20:18

They buried Jesus in a garden in which a brand new tomb had been cut. It's a gathering of several people from his story.

Joseph of Arimathea moves from being a secret disciple to risking everything. The account in Matthew's Gospel (27:57) describes him as a 'rich man'. This has led some scholars to identify him with the rich young man in 19:16–22 who goes away grieving when Jesus tells him to sell his possessions and give the money to the poor, but of course we have no way of verifying the suggestion.

In the garden there is also Nicodemus (19:39), who first came to Jesus under cover of night but now comes in the open, laden with ointments and spices to prepare the body for burial. As night approaches again, this garden is a place of sorrow and hopelessness.

According to John, the garden is also the place where the crucifixion took place (v. 41). Here there are echoes of the first garden, the garden of Eden, and many medieval sculptures and paintings of the crucifixion place a skull and crossbones at the base of the cross, indicating the traditional belief that this was also the burial place of Adam. It is the place of death and new life, redemption, atonement and resurrection.

When Mary Magdalene is called by name (20:16) and recognises the 'gardener's' identity, the place turns on an axis, changing from a garden of sorrow to one of immense joy.

Whereas Adam and Eve were banished from the garden, here in this garden Mary Magdalene, the loved and forgiven one, is given her paradise moment. She becomes the first apostle, carrying the news that she has 'seen the Lord' (v. 18).

There will be gardens and parks in each of our lives that are tabernacles of different memories. There may be places of remembered joy, delight and contentment, but there may also be places where we received bad news, were let down or hurt, or found that the burdens we carried were too heavy. How can we turn these gardens of our lives into places of joy?

Guidelines

'God writes the gospel, not in the Bible alone, but also on trees, and in the flowers and clouds and stars' (attributed to Martin Luther, *The Harper Religious and Inspirational Quotation Companion*, p. 120). John Calvin (1509–64) famously wrote about the created world as God's 'most beautiful theatre', where 'in every part of the world, he has written and as it were engraven the glory of his power, goodness and eternity' (*Opera Selecta* 9:273). What is your reflection upon these words?

The *Benedicite Omnia Opera* is a canticle used in the Book of Common Prayer at Matins. Changes to the Anglican liturgy mean that it is much less often read than it used to be. It is a wonderful song of praise for creation and repeats phrases in a style such as 'Bless the Lord you springs: bless the Lord you seas and rivers; bless the Lord you whales and all that swim in the waters: sing his praise and exalt him for ever.'

In New Zealand a local Benedicite has been written, which speaks of the stars of the southern sky, and the local animals—dolphins, kiwi, hawk and sea lion. Have a go at writing your own Benedicite for the place where you live, including your local natural features, flora and fauna.

Lord, let me walk with you,
into your creation,
putting my steps in Jesus' steps
and entering his rhythm of life,
so that I might see creation more as you see it
and tread more gently upon the landscapes of the earth
as I journey on in the power of the Spirit. Amen.

FURTHER READING

Frédéric Gros, *A Philosophy of Walking*, Verso, 2015.

Belden C. Lane, *The Solace of Fierce Landscapes: Exploring desert and mountain spirituality*, Oxford University Press, 2007.

Margaret Silf, *Sacred Spaces: Stations on a Celtic way*, Lion, 2014.

Graham Usher, *Places of Enchantment: Meeting God in landscapes*, SPCK, 2012.

Deuteronomy

The title 'Deuteronomy' originates from the Greek translation of the Old Testament known as the Septuagint, where the expression 'a copy of this law' (17:18) was translated into Greek as 'this second law' (*deuteronomium*). In the Hebrew Bible, the title of the book , as in the other books of the Torah, is taken from its opening sentence, which starts with 'These are the words'.

The theme of 'these words', given by Moses to a new generation that was about to enter the promised land, shapes the entire structure and theology of the book. There are three speeches (Deuteronomy 1:6—4:40; chs 5—28; 29:1—30:20), and the style in which they are delivered is unique to the book of Deuteronomy, giving it an exhortatory, warm and sermonic character.

The book of Deuteronomy has generated an overwhelming amount of scholarly commentary. Its social, literary and theological content seems to be pregnant with hints that are often exploited by scholars to formulate hypotheses on how the Pentateuch was shaped through the centuries.

A full engagement with these views will be beyond the scope of these notes. However, it is worth observing that most scholars see Deuteronomy as a recasting of the law for a new generation who needed to rediscover, contextualise or experience their past. This gives the book a more theological approach to the law, similar to the Gospel of John in relation to the Synoptic Gospels.

As we delve deeper, I hope that we can reflect on the same task of recasting the biblical message for a new generation.

Quotations are taken from the New Revised Standard Version of the Bible.

16–22 January

1 The first speech (1)

Deuteronomy 1:1–8, 19–21; 2:1–5; 3:23–29

The first verses situate Moses' discourses at the end of the 40 years of wandering in the desert, on the east bank of the Jordan, where the people of Israel were camping as described at the end of the book of Numbers.

Moses' first speech (1:6—4:40) serves as a prologue to the ten commandments. The content has a retrospective element (1:6—3:29), followed by an exhortation as it reflects on past events (4:1–40). The main theme of the speech is obedience to God's orders and its implications for Israel.

The author gives two examples of God's orders, which are stylistically similar and summarise turning points in their journey. The first is found in 1:6–7 ('You have stayed long enough… Go into the hill country') and the second in 2:3 ('You have been skirting this hill country long enough. Head north'). Both orders, when they were first given, were tasking Israel to set in motion their entrance into the promised land. The first was given in the early years of their journey, and led to events of disobedience and punishment. The second was given during the last years of their wandering, and led to events of obedience and victory over enemies.

It is interesting that the same Hebrew expression, *rav lakha*, literally 'enough of you', appears in both orders and is also included in the answer that God gives to Moses' pleas in 3:26. This seems to give the impression of an impatient God, which has perplexed many commentators, especially when it occurs in response to Moses' prayer. Some rabbis have tried to soften the abruptness by offering a different interpretation of the phrase in 3:26—for example, 'too much for you' or 'a master for you'.

However, if we keep in mind that Deuteronomy was shaped by key turning points in the history of Israel, through this portrayal of impatience we could hear echoes of a God challenging present and future generations that face an urgent need for social-religious reforms. He is saying, 'Enough of lingering in your status quo; enough of your pious pleas. It is time to act, be obedient and take hold of the land that God has already given you.'

2 The first speech (2)

Deuteronomy 4:1–5, 9–19, 25–26, 32–40

Having recapped the journey so far in terms of disobedience and obedience, Moses now exhorts the Israelites to see their future well-being in the light of keeping God's law. The connection between the land and obedience to God's law becomes an important topic in the book of Deuteronomy. While it is linked with the unbroken promise given to the patriarchs (1:8; 4:37–38), there is also a subtle conditional clause for the current and future generations (4:25–26, 40).

Weinfeld suggests that, here, Deuteronomy is merging two ancient Near Eastern concepts of covenant and treaty. On one side is the 'royal grant', through which a king grants gifts freely to his subjects, and on the other is the 'vassal treaty', which constitutes a covenant based on the obligations of a subject. In merging them, Deuteronomy portrays a God who can speak passionately of his unconditional relationship with Israel based on love for the patriarchs and, at the same time, can withdraw his favour if Israel fails to keep his law. This theological framework becomes key for the following historical books in explaining the tension between the eternal promises given to David's dynasty and the exile that followed its failure.

Of all the obligations of the covenant, avoidance of idolatry is emphasised the most (vv. 15–19, 25–28), and Moses draws on memories of the divine theophany at Sinai (called Horeb in Deuteronomy) to reinforce it. Despite the fact that only a few of the current generation would have been present at Sinai, perhaps as children, they are now all portrayed as actually standing, seeing and hearing the entire theophany. This fusion of experiences across generations reflects the significant role that the passing on of memories played in ancient cultures, as well as the biblical understanding of past and future generations as one body, sharing the same communal memories and experiences. As the Mishnah puts it, 'In every generation one must view oneself as if he came out of Egypt… It was not only our ancestors that the Holy One redeemed, but us, too, with them.'

The rooting of theology in communal memory is a crucial element in the Old Testament and in Jewish thinking. In the words of Abraham Heschel, a Jewish theologian and philospher of the 20th century, 'The essence of Jewish religious thinking does not lie in entertaining a concept of God but in the ability to articulate a memory of moments of illumination by His presence. Israel is not a people of definers but a people of witnesses' (in Tigay, p. 46).

3 The second speech: the ten commandments

The second speech continues the process of engaging the communal memory of the current generation by setting them at Sinai/Horeb, listening to the ten commandments being given. While the rest of the law is said to be given separately through Moses as intermediary, the ten commandments are emphasised as being heard by the entire community directly from God (vv. 22–24). This is an important element in establishing their authority and uniqueness.

Throughout ancient Near Eastern codes of law, the king is seen as the originator of law. Divine beings are often mentioned in the prologue to written laws, but they play a lesser role, mostly as helpers in establishing the rule of a king, or as commissioners advising the king as he brings justice to the land. The Old Testament is unique in claiming a direct connection between its law and a divine utterance. This reflects the conviction that God is the king of Israel, hence also its legislator.

The unique delivery of the ten commandments is described as a terrifying experience in which people feared for their lives (vv. 24–26), but there is a subtle difference between its portrayals in Exodus and Deuteronomy. In Exodus 20:20, the fear of the Lord following the theophany is said to be (in the Hebrew) 'on the faces' of the people. (A similar expression is used in Deuteronomy 2:25 to describe the terror of the nations when facing Israel.) However, Deuteronomy 5:29 internalises the fear, saying that it is inside their heart (translated as 'mind' in NRSV.) A similar wordplay is used by Jeremiah 32:39–40 to signal a deep devotion.

The ten commandments are among the most well-known verses of the Bible, but can you enumerate them? This might not be as easy as you think. The exact division has been interpreted differently by different traditions. So, according to Philo and Josephus, the ten commandments cover (1) monotheism; (2) idolatry; (3) false oaths; (4) sabbath; (5) honouring parents; (6) murder; (7) adultery; (8) theft; (9) false witness; (10) covetousness. This division is mentioned by the Church Fathers and is followed by the Protestant and Eastern Orthodox Churches. However, Augustine combined numbers 1 and 2 as the first commandment, while splitting the last into two separate commandments. This is the order followed now by the Catholic and Lutheran Churches. Meanwhile, the Jewish tradition sees the opening statement, 'I am the Lord your God' (v. 6), as the first commandment, and combines numbers 1 and 2 as the second commandment.

4 Hear, O Israel

Deuteronomy 6

As soon as the ten commandments have been given at Mount Sinai, the focus is shifted back to Moab, with the people waiting to enter the promised land. The shift is introduced subtly while a natural connection is maintained with the theophany in Sinai. The very same 'commandments, statutes and ordinances' that God told Moses at Sinai (5:31) are now elaborated at Moab in front of another generation (6:1). As we have already noted, the fusion of different generations' experiences and the different emphases that they might bring to the law becomes important for the whole book of Deuteronomy. Any new perspective or new light shone on to the Law is justified as being part of the original experience in Sinai and, as such, carries the same authority.

One particular aspect that Deuteronomy brings afresh is its rejection of any form of idolatry and the need for sole devotion to Yahweh. This emphasis is captured by verses 4–5, which in the Jewish tradition is called the *Shema* (from the first Hebrew words of 'Hear, O Israel'). These verses are considered to be the most important part of Jewish liturgy. They are taught to a child as soon as it learns to speak; they are recited in the morning and evening prayers, when one is resting in bed or on one's deathbed, or before martyrdom.

In Jewish liturgy, the *Shema* is interpreted as a pledge of loyalty before God, or, as rabbis called it, accepting 'the yoke of the kingship of heaven'. As Weinfeld has demonstrated, this liturgical approach fits well with the original context of a treaty through which kings would make demands on their subjects, regarding their sole kingship and instruction of children. An Assyrian treaty illustrates the point: 'You shall love Ashurbanipal, King of Assyria, as you love yourselves… You shall instruct your sons who will live in the future… you shall not set over yourselves another king, another lord.' According to Weinfeld, even the language of loving God with all our heart, soul and strength should be understood in a similar context: the king demands our entire loyalty (heart), even to the point of giving our life (soul), while putting into his service all that we possess (strength).

How does our devotion to God compare with these demands?

5 The threat to loyalty

Deuteronomy 7:1–6; 9:4–7, 15–19; 10:12–22

After describing the degree of loyalty that is required by God, as captured by the *Shema*, Moses draws attention in chapters 7—11 to the threats that Israel's faith and loyalty will face as it enters the promised land. Chapter 7 is concerned with the lure of the Canaanites' idolatry, chapter 8 points to the temptation of being too self-reliant and chapters 9—10 touch on the theme of seeing one's own righteousness as the reason for the success achieved. Thematically these chapters are constructed as a response to a potential misjudgement by Israel of its own experience and history (7:17; 8:17; 9:4).

One of the most striking aspects of these warnings is the command to annihilate the entire people of Canaan (7:2). The Hebrew phrase *herem*, often translated as 'ban' or 'utterly destroy', refers to the ancient practice of total annihilation as a sacrifice to a divine being. Feeling the harshness of the command, some rabbis have tried to soften its meaning by interpreting it as a last resort against nations that refused the terms of peace. Others have argued that the prohibition of intermarriage in the very next verse suggests that the command could have not meant total destruction. Some scholars see the ban in Deuteronomy as a theoretical or utopian statement, perhaps added later in retrospect, that was never put into practice (as hinted by 1 Kings 9:20–21). Whatever the case, it is interesting that Deuteronomy removes any hint that the ban constitutes a sacrifice to the Lord. Rather, the severity of the command aims to stop the spread of idolatry and has no ethnic boundaries. The same treatment threatens the people of Israel if they themselves introduce idolatry (13:13–16).

The lack of a sacrificial element is also evident in the retelling of Israel's rebellion in worshipping the golden calf (chs 9—10). The book of Exodus concludes the same story with the erection of the tabernacle (chs 35—40), as a restorative step that brought God's presence back into the community; Deuteronomy concludes it with a call to a personal and passionate fulfilment of the law (10:12–22). This shift of focus from rituals to devotion is an important perspective in the book and can be spotted in many parallel narratives.

6 Obedience

Deuteronomy 11

We now reach the end of what has been a lengthy introduction to the main body of the law, which will be covered in chapters 12—26. Chapter 11 homes in on the same theme of obedience that has already been touched on by the previous chapters. Its emphasis on obedience is reflected by the colourful language that urges Israel to 'walk in his ways', to love him, to serve him, to keep all his commandments and to hold fast to him. The motivation for such devotion is described in three main paragraphs.

First, verses 1–9 refer to the great deeds that the Lord did in the past—but only the punitive acts are mentioned, in Egypt and in the wilderness. Having witnessed the Lord's discipline, the current generation is in a better position to understand the importance of obedience.

Second, verses 10–21 refer to the fact that prosperity in the promised land, unlike in Egypt, depends not on human endeavour but on God's favour in providing the necessary rain. Egypt received very little rain during the year. Its irrigation came from the flooding of the Nile, which was caused by melting snow during the summer or the spring rains at its sources in Ethiopia. A system of canals and reservoirs was developed to channel the excess water into the fields. The uniqueness of this situation was recognised by the ancient Egyptians, and they looked down on foreign lands that required rain (which they referred to as a 'Nile in the sky'). The rabbis often discussed whether or not the promised land was truly a better land than Egypt. Although they concluded that it was, they also recognised its vulnerability. Its superiority was beyond any human control and rested solely on God's favour, making it, in the words of Rabbi Rashbam, 'a land worse than all other lands to those who do not observe God's commands'.

Third, verses 22–25 refer to the promise of military victory in expelling any nation that would resist Israel's advance. While this echoes the promise of victory already given in previous chapters (for example, 9:1–5), it now makes success dependent on Israel's obedience.

The entire exhortation is concluded with a declaration of choice between blessing and curse. The same theme is taken up again at the end of the book, after the whole law has been expounded.

Guidelines

One of the striking elements of the book of Deuteronomy is the warmth of the first eleven chapters, where we are constantly encouraged to be obedient and keep the commandments of our Lord. Throughout these chapters, God's love for Israel, his care and devotion are portrayed with strong emotive language. The same intensity of devotion is repeatedly requested from Israel in return. It is interesting to note that at the heart of this passionate relationship between the Lord and Israel stands the law.

We, however, can be timid about placing love and the law side by side. Often we like to excuse God of any 'legalistic' misunderstandings so that his love can be more visible.

The book of Deuteronomy reminds us how genuine devotion can truly reflect a passionate God as well as a deep sense of obedience. In this covenantal relationship, love is greater than mere sentiment and laws are an earthly expression of divine love.

Deuteronomy often brings a new light or emphasis for its generation, but always sees itself as originating from the same encounter in Sinai. There are hints of innovation but they are deeply rooted in the ongoing tradition. Perhaps we may reflect on how we can replicate Deuteronomy's task of contextualising the biblical message for today's generation.

1 Place of worship

Deuteronomy 12:1–20, 26–27

Chapters 12—26 present us with a corpus of laws that constitute the main content of the book. To cover the entire collection of laws would be beyond the scope of these notes. Instead we shall emphasise those laws that show unique elements of Deuteronomistic interpretation.

The first law to be mentioned addresses the issue of worship. After rejecting the religious practices of the other nations, Deuteronomy sets a centralised agenda, such that the entire sacrificial system is performed in one location. This is one of the most distinctive laws introduced by the book of Deuteronomy. The practice of offering sacrifices in various locations had been common in Israel since the days of the patriarchs and continued even after Israel entered the promised land. Deuteronomy seems to have considered the practice to be provisional until the land was captured and secured (vv. 9–11), in order to allow for the safety of the people as they travelled from distant places. However, we only encounter attempts to centralise the sacrificial system during the reigns of Hezekiah and Josiah (2 Kings 18:4, 22; chs. 22—23). This is one of the main reasons why attempts to date the book of Deuteronomy often bring into discussion the reforms of these two kings, asking whether their reforms were influenced by the theology of Deuteronomy or vice versa.

The rationale behind this law has also perplexed scholars, especially as it would have been a very disruptive reform. Rather than increasing devotion, limiting sacrifice to a distant location would have diminished most people's religious experience and the livelihood of many Levites. Many reasons have been proposed—for example, the promotion of national unity, or worship uniformity as a response to outside religious or political threats. One of the most fascinating explanations, in my opinion, follows the line of the medieval rabbi Maimonides, who saw the introduction of the law as a way to minimise the sacrificial system of the day. Many scholars agree that in Deuteronomy we find a shift from a sacrificial cult to an affection for the law. The centralisation would have served the same agenda of curtailing popular sacrifices. The religious gap left as a result of this, as Tigay suggests (p. 119), would have been filled by prayer and the study of the law, which seems to resonate with the overall theme of Deuteronomy.

2 Remission of debt

Deuteronomy 15

The law concerning the remission of debts is found in the middle of a sequence of worship-related laws. This should not be surprising. Ancient scribes often organised a set of unrelated laws as a chain of ideas in which a wordplay or motif served as a thread that held the series together. In this instance, the topic of periodical rituals or offerings in relation to worship holds these laws together. After establishing the place of worship and excluding idolatrous practices (chs 13—14), the author moves into the rituals that are to be observed periodically. So we have a tithe every year, a poor-tithe every third year (ch. 14), the remission of debts every seventh year, the firstlings every year (ch. 15) and the pilgrimage festival three times a year (ch. 16).

The observance of the seventh year, or sabbatical year, finds parallels in different parts of Exodus 21—23 and in Leviticus 25. However, these passages speak only of the release of slaves and the fallowing of the land. The remission of debts as described by Deuteronomy only appears in what Leviticus calls the Jubilee, which happened in the 50th year, not the seventh.

There have been a few attempts to synchronise these two approaches. Some scholars have suggested that the remission of debts happened on both occasions. This would, however, make the Jubilee less significant. Others have suggested that the Hebrew verb *samat* should be understood as deferment rather than remission. This means that every seventh year there would be a time of debt relief, during which no payments would be made for debts. Payments would then resume in the following year. This cycle would run until the 50th year of Jubilee.

Another view is to see Deuteronomy as a later development, which extends the fallowing of the land to include personal debts. By shortening the period for debt remission, Deuteronomy would have brought greater relief for individuals. In Leviticus, this relief would have mostly benefited the families or the children of the debtor.

Whichever interpretation is followed, it is clear that Deuteronomy envisages a nation where economic policies serve the social fabric. The creditor and debtor are bound together by an agreement that should reflect God's covenant and promises of rest.

3 Leadership

Deuteronomy 16:18–20; 17:8–20; 18:15–16
In these chapters, the author covers four types of authorities that regulate different aspects of social and religious life: judges, kings, priests and prophets. This account of dispersed authority seems to envisage a society with no single authoritarian figure or system. Great attention is given to the limiting of their powers, and this is most noticeable in the description of the role of the king—the individual likely to become the most powerful.

The description of the king's role (17:14–20) is different from the other three in that it makes no mention of his rights or authority, although he is permitted to have his own copy of the law to study. While Deuteronomy offers a more accepting view of the monarchy than the books of Samuel, it still limits its office, especially its military and economic power, together with its diplomatic endeavours. Above all, it sets the king under the law. He is to deepen his wisdom and devotion through the study of God's laws. This would have stood in contrast to the ancient Near Eastern view, already mentioned, in which monarchs were seen as the originators of laws. Their legislative power often served to propagate their prestige, displaying their wisdom or unique relationship with the gods. So Hammurabi often spoke proudly of his laws in terms of 'my statutes', 'my justice' and 'my words, which I wrote'.

The image of a humble king, however, seems to have been utopian; it was never realised during the history of Israel's monarchy. The reality showed an ongoing competition for power. This tension between the reality and the ideal gave rise to the role of the prophets, who served as God's spokesmen and critics. The prophets, according to Greenberg (p. 112), 'mercilessly exposed the gap between ideal and reality, but did not offer a reconciliation'. It was the later development of Judaism, from the Hasmonean dynasty to Phariseeism, that tried to offer a political synthesis of the vision, and it was in this context that the Christian interpretation of a messianic king grew up. This view encompasses both the figure of a humble king and that of a prophet who continues to challenge the reality of existing powers (Acts 3:22; 7:37).

4 Family laws

Deuteronomy 21:10–21; 22:13–30

This collection of laws is concerned with various aspects of personal, family and community life. Some of them are hard to digest from our perspective, serving as prime examples of those aspects of the law that can unsettle us. The social and cultural gap that exists between us and the original audience can lead us to represent these laws as barbaric, inexplicable or unbearable.

However, digging deeper, we can see that although they are clearly addressing social tensions that arise from a predominantly masculine and violent society, they are attempting to bring protection for the marginalised. This protection is achieved by curbing the extent of the liberty that a man can exercise. Later, the rabbis went further with this explanation by pointing out that some of the laws do not place a sanction on the actions described but attempt to discourage them. So, according to Rashi, the grouping of the laws concerning the captive wife, firstborn and disobedient child is not accidental. Together, they alert the reader to the situations that would arise as a series of consequences from marriage to a captive wife. The husband will despise her, leading to a situation where the children grow up being rebellious, resulting in family trauma.

The death penalty for a disobedient son or for a young woman who is found to have lost her virginity is also understood as an attempt to discourage rather than as a sanction. Rabbis and some modern scholars see this harsh penalty as rhetorical, serving for educational purposes but never intended to be carried out. Similarly harsh penalties are observed in other ancient Mesopotamian contracts and treaties and are believed never to have been carried out.

The evaluation of these kinds of laws from a contemporary perspective displays a mixed picture. On one hand, some scholars (such as Weinfeld) point out the humanitarian agenda that Deuteronomy applies in recasting these laws when compared with the social context. This is noticed in the bias that Deuteronomy shows towards the rights of the marginalised at the expense of the powerful. Others, including Brueggemann, wonder if Deuteronomy went far enough in challenging a patriarchal society. According to him, the rawness of these laws, although positive for their ancient times, reflect an unfinished process of fully respecting human dignity.

5 The assembly of the Lord

Deuteronomy 23:1–15

Deuteronomy describes the people of Israel as a chosen people who are wholly devoted to God. The question of who does and who doesn't belong to this community therefore has an important place within the legal and covenant framework of Deuteronomy. The question is answered by excluding three categories:

- People who have mutilated their body, especially in the form of castration (v. 1). This was a well-known practice in the ancient Near East and was recognised in connection with official roles—for example, the role of the eunuch. The Israelites' preoccupation with emasculation could have reflected a natural concern for fertility, as an important guarantee of genetic continuity.
- Children of an illicit relationship (v. 2). This is often understood as children born out of wedlock, but the meaning of the Hebrew word *mamzer* is uncertain. Talmud links it with 22:30 and understands it as meaning the offspring of incestuous intercourse. The Septuagint translates it as the offspring of a prostitute, while others see it as a general term for foreigners.
- Ammonites, Moabites, Edomites and Egyptians (vv. 3, 7–8). The exclusion of Ammonites and Moabites is based on the claim that they were inhospitable towards the Israelites as they escaped from Egypt.

On the last point, it is perplexing to note that Egypt is treated more tolerantly, despite having been the main oppressor. This has led scholars to suggest that perhaps the exclusion list based on ethnicity relates instead to international tensions during a particular period in Israel's history. While it would be difficult to speculate on the exact historical context, it is true that the issue of exclusion becomes more complex as we progress through the history of the Old Testament. So, the book of Ruth (who was, herself, a Moabite) seems to provide a more generous interpretation of the restriction, whereas Nehemiah follows a stricter path (Nehemiah 13:1–3, 23–30). Isaiah 56:3–8 seems to set a new vision for the future in which eunuchs and foreigners are welcomed into God's covenant. This messianic vision takes expression in the early church in their acceptance of the Gentiles.

However, the question of exclusion, whether in doctrinal or canonical terms, has continued to be a burning issue throughout church history. Ignoring it or being too simplistic about it will mean that we fail to take the biblical approach seriously. We need to continue to wrestle with the same issue expressed in different contexts.

6 First fruits

Deuteronomy 26

The main corpus of the law is now concluded with a liturgical declaration that the farmer is to recite as he brings the first fruits to the place that the Lord has chosen (vv. 1–11). There is a striking parallelism between this last law and the first law stated in chapter 12, concerning the place chosen by the Lord where the offerings and tithes were to be brought. The entire law is thus initiated and concluded with an act of worship. The encompassing element of worship is noticed as the farmer retells the whole history of Israel through the lens of thanksgiving as he presents his first fruits. Deuteronomy turns a rite about the fertility of the land into a historical reflection. The Lord is worshipped not only because of the immediate control that he exercises over the natural elements that made these fruits grow, but because, through his control of history, he has given the land to the people in the first place.

As Tigay points out, this shift of thanksgiving, from immediate experience towards meditative history, shapes the Jewish liturgy even today. So, in 'Blessing after meals', thanksgiving for food is followed by thanksgiving for the land, covenant, Torah and other historical acts of kindness.

The historical reflection presented in Deuteronomy is never seen as distant and irrelevant. This farmer and all who come after him, throughout the centuries, will declare annually, 'Today… I have come into the land… So now I bring the first of the fruit of the ground that you, O Lord, have given me' (vv. 3, 10). As we noticed in previous chapters, Deuteronomy continually fuses the experience of present and future generations. This living participation in God's salvific history, as experienced in the act of worship, is what sustains and motivates obedience to God's commandments.

As the farmer celebrates the fruit of the land, he has also to remember the landless (Levites, foreigners, orphans and widows) by offering the poor-tithe every three years. Only then can he claim that he has kept the commandments fully, and pray for blessing on all the people of Israel (vv. 12–14).

Guidelines

When reading a collection of Old Testament laws, it is natural for us to wonder about their relevance to our lives. Very often, the law is treated in spiritual terms in relation to grace, but when we consider whether any application can be drawn for our own social or ethical context, we become aware of the interpretative challenge that the law poses. How can we apply it today?

This question is relevant not only for the ten commandments, but also for those aspects that might seem too utopian, too harsh, or based on the complex demands of a sacrificial system. Some have attempted to answer it by classifying the Old Testament laws into three categories—moral, civil and ceremonial—and then arguing that while the ceremonial aspects no longer carry authority, we should try to apply either the moral or the civil aspects, or both. This could be helpful to some degree, but the laws show a more organic unity of these three elements, making the proposed division artificial at times. Think, for example, about the law concerning the remission of debt.

What the book of Deuteronomy achieved for its generation can serve as a framework for our approach to the law. Deuteronomy interprets the law for a new generation, making use of the ancient Near Eastern concept of covenant or treaty. In doing so, it brings new emphases and reflects some of its generation's political and religious concerns. We find hints of innovation in Deuteronomy, although they are deeply rooted in the ongoing tradition.

As we engage with the law, we may reinterpret it through the new covenant found in Christ, in whom the entire law is fulfilled. So, rather than deciding what parts are relevant, we treat it as a whole, trying to understand its values, principles and paradigms and to apply them through the new covenant in Christ. The task is not easy; as we have seen, Deuteronomy introduces further complexities when it engages with the same interpretative task.

Reflect on some aspects of the law and think about how they can shape our social responsibilities. How does the covenant in Christ enable us to reinterpret them?

1   Renewing the covenant

Deuteronomy 27

Chapter 27 describes a series of ceremonies that the people of Israel will perform at Mount Ebal and Mount Gerezim as they enter the promised land. This seems to constitute a covenant ritual, as it shows many similarities to the covenant ceremony described in Exodus 24 after Moses had conveyed God's laws at Sinai.

The description of this covenant ritual, to be performed once they are inside the promised land, is interrupted in verses 9–10 by a solemn declaration that 'this very day' they have become the people of the Lord. These verses refer to the current covenant being established in the land of Moab before the people enter the promised land. In fact, the whole of chapter 27 seems to disrupt the flow of events between the end of chapter 26 and chapter 28, which speaks of the covenant established in

Moab after the entire law had been conveyed (see 29:1).

The interplay of these public declarations seems to set the covenant in the promised land in the light of the covenant in Moab, which in turn was a renewal of the covenant at Sinai. This theological unity and continuity between the covenants of the past, present and future is crucial to the understanding set forth by Deuteronomy. It serves as a framework to bring together old and new declarations as aspects of the same covenant. It also brings the past to life, such that God's covenant continues to be renewed and encountered in and through every crucial moment of history. This process of renewal brings a fusion of the various generations, so that 'this very day' is experienced by everyone despite the generation gap.

An interesting aspect of the ceremonies to be carried out inside the promised land is the series of curses. Although we are told that the ceremony contains words of both blessing and curse (vv. 12–13), we are given only the words of the curse. Some scholars have argued that the blessing is implied. Others have suggested that the curses mentioned here are not part of the blessing–curse dichotomy described in chapter 28; instead, they belong to a third and final declaration after the people have publicly declared their acceptance of the covenant. The mention of 'secrecy' in verses 15 and 24 seems to suggest that the curses were meant as a warning to those who might publicly accept the covenant but secretly reject it.

2 Blessings and curses

Deuteronomy 28:1–19, 25–33

Chapter 28 follows on from the content of chapter 26, where the people of Israel were preparing to accept the Lord's covenant after hearing the whole of the law. The list of blessings and curses is then presented as an encouragement and warning concerning the consequences of keeping or not keeping God's covenant.

It has been observed that many ancient Near Eastern covenants, treaties, agreements and loyalty oaths concluded with a similar series of blessings and curses. In fact, Deuteronomy shares many features with this common literary genre. For example, these agreements all devote more space to the curses than the blessings, and cover a wide and similar range of social, economic and political events. The similarities sometimes run very close. The order of themes covered in verses 26–33 (carcasses as food for animals, skin inflammation, madness, blindness, dismay, rape, loss of possessions and the plundering of children) is almost identical to the order of curses found in the vassal treaty of Esarhaddon, a king of Assyria during the seventh century BC. The adaptation of well-known literary contents could explain the presence of such macabre threats. This is not to diminish the intent behind the warnings; however, it is important to evaluate them within the appropriate context.

Any common material has clearly been reworked, however, to reflect Israel's distinctive faith and history. For example, in contrast to other ancient treaties, there is mention of only one divine being who is responsible for all the blessings and the curses. Israel's unique identity as God's holy people is reaffirmed among other common blessings (v. 9) and all the calamities culminate in a re-enactment of a unique Jewish experience—that of slavery in Egypt (see v. 68).

This covenantal vision of history through the blessings and the curses makes the people responsible for the choices that they will make in relation to God's laws. Their choices are not neutral or to be taken lightly, as they will have serious consequences for the future. The notion of a covenant also stipulates a second party (in this case, God), outside people's jurisdiction or control, that faithfully watches over their choices. This Deuteronomistic vision becomes an important voice as the history of Israel is unravelled and interpreted in the books of Joshua to Kings.

3 Punishment and renewal

Deuteronomy 29:1–15, 19–25; 30:1–10

These chapters contain Moses' last speech to the people of Israel as he charges them to keep God's covenant. Just as he did in the first chapters, he recapitulates Israel's experience in Egypt and in the wilderness. The exposition of the law is surrounded by an ongoing reflection on God's salvation, power and care. However, as Moses points out, Israel initially failed to understand their significance (29:4). It took 40 years of trials in the wilderness for the people to really know their God (v. 6). The punitive years in the wilderness turned out also to be educative years: as the people now stand to renew God's covenant in Moab, 40 years after the covenant at Sinai, they are in a better position to grasp fully what it means to enter into a covenant relationship with the Lord.

After describing the ceremony of accepting the covenant (vv. 10–14), Moses then warns of individuals who fail to understand the exclusive loyalty that God's covenant requires. Their blindness is pointed out in wordplay as they are portrayed affirming the opposite of what is to befall them. They bless themselves and feel confident while curses and annihilation await (vv. 19–20). Their condemnation is escalated to encompass the entire nation and land, hinting at the calamity of exile.

This is not, however, the end of the covenant. Chapter 30 refers to the hope of renewal if the people turn back to God with all their heart. As a response, the Lord will not only reverse their fate but will also give them a deeper devotion, as described by the circumcision of the heart (v. 6). This echoes the action that the Lord takes in 29:4, opening hearts, eyes and ears that, until this day, have been closed—repeating the cycle of deepening spirituality through the trials of punishment, whether in the wilderness or in exile.

There is a gentle underlying theme in these verses, of a deeper spirituality emerging as the people humble themselves during the trials of punishment. God is the one who ultimately gives it, but the people have to yearn for it through obedience. Without repentance and obedience, the trials remain devastating. Throughout those trials, however, God is waiting faithfully for his people to return and take delight in the blessings of his covenant.

4 Preparing a new leader

Deuteronomy 31:9–30

Chapters 31—34 are often seen as the epilogue to both the book of Deuteronomy and the whole Pentateuch. The author now begins to look beyond Moses to a people who are about to conquer the land under a new leader, Joshua. Various scholars have observed in chapter 31 a series of tensions, contradictions and double retellings in the way this transition of leadership is narrated. It has been argued that the book of Deuteronomy makes use of different existing traditions, which reflect their own unique nuances in the retelling of such an important political and religious moment.

Despite the different layers of sources, however, chapter 31 presents us with a well-structured narrative, laid out in a chiastic pattern:

The law (vv. 9–13)
    The appointment of Joshua (vv. 14–15)
        Request for a song (vv. 16–22)
    The appointment of Joshua (v. 23)
The law (vv. 24–27)

As Tigay has suggested, this shows intentionality, perhaps to unify the various traditions but also, more importantly, to set the task and the field of operation for the new leader. The account of Joshua's appointment is interrupted by God's instruction to Moses to write a song. The content of the song, which is recorded in 32:1–43, is to witness against Israel's future apostasy. This seems to colour the task ahead for Joshua, who, apart from military conquest, will also be required to wrestle with a defiant and rebellious people (see Joshua 24).

Joshua's appointment is surrounded by references to the writing of the law. This seems to set the mandate for his leadership. The same theme will be emphasised again as he takes charge in Joshua 1:7–8. There, Joshua is twice encouraged to be strong and bold, being assured of God's presence and help as he faces his difficult task.

The role of the law is mentioned not only with regard to the future leader. Its place is found also among the common people. Most ancient ritual texts were used solely by a religious or intellectual elite; Deuteronomy, however, opens up the law to everyone, including women, children and foreigners (v. 12). The public reading of the law brings not only spiritual nourishment to the society but also an awareness of the civil rights that individuals and communities enjoy under God's covenant, making leaders more accountable.

5 The song

Deuteronomy 32:1–12, 15–21, 26–27, 36–43

Moses' song, briefly mentioned in the previous chapter, amid the account of Joshua's appointment, is now given in full. The song is meant to stand as a warning sign for future generations. As it is recited on different occasions, its message is expected to bring transformation, just as rain is received and has life-giving effects (vv. 1–3).

The main theme of the song is that of a 'broken faith' between Israel and God. Some scholars have argued that it resembles the genre of a 'covenant lawsuit'. This genre is reflected in other ancient materials, where a suzerain would appeal to the gods to condemn a vassal for not maintaining an agreement. He would enumerate the signs of the vassal's ingratitude and declare war for the betrayal.

Moses' song differs from the genre, however, in that God is presented as both the accuser and the punisher. There is no other divine being that will arbitrate between Israel and God. Heaven and earth are called, as literary devices, to witness that Israel did indeed accept the terms of God's covenant (v. 1; see 4:26; 30:19; 31:28). In setting the case against the nation for breaking the covenant, the song describes Israel as degenerate, false, perverse and crooked (v. 5), in contrast to God who is perfect, just, faithful, without deceit and upright (v. 4).

A turning point in the poem comes with God's decision to restrain his punishment because Israel's enemies would draw the wrong conclusion about the Lord himself (vv. 26–27). This idea is expanded in the following verses, giving hope for a reinstatement of Israel.

Throughout the song, God is portrayed as watching passionately over his relationship with Israel, always taking the initiative and punishing the people's unfaithfulness. Hence, a covenant with the Lord, in Moses' words, 'is no trifling matter for you, but rather your very life' (32:47). Yet a ray of hope does flow from God's commitment to the relationship—a commitment that transcends Israel's response. God chose his people well before they were able to respond as a nation (vv. 8–9; despite textual variants in ancient and modern translations of v. 8, the theme of divine election is consistent). Even when Israel responds negatively to his covenant, God remains faithful and restrains his punishment, because of his glory.

6 The death of Moses

Deuteronomy 32:48–52; 34:1–12

The book of Deuteronomy and, with it, the whole Pentateuch ends with a brief narrative on Moses' death. The first section, in 32:48–52, seems to echo a similar narrative in Numbers 27:12–14. The beginning of Deuteronomy touched briefly on the fate of Moses (1:37, 3:26; 4:21), but explained his exclusion from the promised land as being 'on account of' the people. Some scholars have suggested that these verses are trying to portray Moses' exclusion in a more positive light, as a vicarious punishment. However, at the end, other traditions of the Pentateuch are incorporated, making Moses more personally accountable (32:51).

Nevertheless, what we might call Moses' 'failure' does not overshadow his legacy. He is praised as an unequalled prophet (34:11) because of his unique relationship with God and the miracles that he performed through the years. This would probably explain the fact that his tomb was left unknown. Moses' prestige could have attracted unorthodox piety towards his figure, even beyond his death, leading to the breaking of God's commandments, as in the story of Saul's attempt to raise the spirit of Samuel (1 Samuel 28).

There is a humbling undertone throughout this account of Moses' last days. Despite the enormous achievement of leading an entire nation from slavery to the promised land, he continues to be seen as a mere servant of the Lord, obeying God's commands even if it means never tasting the fruit of his work and dying alone. His willingness to labour for the benefit of another generation is a remarkable characteristic of Moses' leadership.

Joshua, as the leader for a new stage in Israel's history, is shown as continuing from within the same Mosaic tradition. He represents a new era, a new context where the 'little ones' (1:39) have grown up and are taking charge. Yet he is to share in the same spirit of wisdom as previous leaders. This transition *and* continuity of teaching is what the book of Deuteronomy has been working towards throughout its pages. It makes Deuteronomy, in the words of Brueggemann (p. 291), 'in the end, powerfully contemporary for every generation that finds itself pondering old miracles, trusting old memories, heeding old commands, and always again entering new territory of promise (see Hebrews 11:39–40)'.

Guidelines

The emphatic language employed in the last section of Deuteronomy, encouraging and warning us to be faithful and obedient to God's covenant, stands as a reminder that the God of our faith is active and passionate. He is not a passive object of our piety. He intervenes, bringing blessings and curses. This vision of divine intervention as defined in a covenant relationship can be unsettling for our lives today—and understandably so, especially when we are confronted with a simplistic interpretation of why, for example, a particular calamity has occurred. The same unease is evident in some later books of the Bible, including many of the Psalms, as well as the book of Job, who wrestles with the same theme of punishment and blessing in relation to his righteousness.

These ancient writers never saw the experience of suffering as an excuse to remove God from the equation, even if it meant making God accountable for his promises. It is in the light of this that we turn to reflect on the role that God plays in our lives. How often do we bring God into the equation when making decisions for ourselves or for the surrounding community? Spend some time in silence to think about key decisions to be made in your life. Bring them before God in prayer, whether with praise or repentance, being assured that we always have a faithful God.

FURTHER READING

J.H. Tigay, *The JPS Torah Commentary: Deuteronomy*, Jewish Publication Society, 1996.

M. Weinfeld, *Deuteronomy 1—11: A new translation with introduction and commentary* (The Anchor Bible), Yale University Press, 2008.

D.L. Christensen, *Deuteronomy 1—21:9* (Word Biblical Commentary), Thomas Nelson, 2001.

W. Brueggemann, *Deuteronomy* (Abingdon Old Testament Commentaries), Abingdon Press, 2001.

M. Greenberg, 'Biblical attitudes toward power' in B.E. Firmage (ed.), *Religion and Law: Biblical-Judaic and Islamic perspectives*, Eisenbrauns, 1990.

Matthew 15—18

A careful examination of the Gospel of Matthew reveals that it is divided into five sections. Its contents are designed to correspond with the first five books of the Hebrew scriptures, the so-called 'Torah' (meaning 'Instruction') or 'Books of Moses'. Within Judaism these are the holiest and most authoritative volumes of the scriptures. Meditation upon them is continually encouraged within those scriptures themselves. It is no surprise, then, that Matthew should be the first book within the canon of New Testament scriptures.

It is entirely mistaken to regard the books of Moses as a series of commands issued by a despotic deity, which are to be blindly followed. Rather, they set out the reality of God, God's people, God's purpose and God's word and invite those who trust in God to live freely within the space that they provide. So it is with Matthew's Gospel. Here we are presented with Jesus as God's transformative Messiah, with his ways, his acts, his parables and his teaching. These provide the framework within which we may learn to live as his followers. There is certainly a call to obedience, but, even more so, the inspiration to live freely, responsibly, creatively and faithfully according to what we have come to know of Christ.

Jesus was not, and is not, predictable. All our efforts to domesticate him and make him conform to what we think a Messiah ought to be are doomed to fail. Jesus is not a plastic figure that we can mould or distort to our desired shape. He is what he is and exists objectively over against us. In the Apostles' Creed, for all its importance, the life and ministry of Jesus are passed over too swiftly, swallowed up by a comma in between 'born of the Virgin Mary' and 'suffered under Pontius Pilate'. This cannot be right, and our readings in Matthew provide an opportunity to give proper space to the saving and ennobling life of Christ. It is hard to do him justice, and it should be no surprise that there are four Gospels, enabling us to hear him quadrophonically and view him from differing angles. Matthew's Gospel, the longest of the four, gives us a sustained view of a character who does not disappoint.

Quotations are taken from the New Revised Standard Version except where otherwise indicated.

1 The true law

Matthew 15:1–9

Readers of the Gospels swiftly discover that Jesus argued frequently with the Pharisees and scribes. The Pharisees were a strict, largely lay movement within the Judaism of Jesus' day, and the scribes associated with them were among the elite who could write and were therefore experts in the law of Moses. The irony is that Jesus would have had much in common with them, but often it is the case that those who are closest to each other argue with one another the most. The Pharisees sought to take regulations that applied to the temple and extend them to the ordinary household, thus supposedly sanctifying the whole of life. This was the case with the stipulation that hands should be washed before eating (v. 2): it originally applied to priests and the sacrificial offerings (Leviticus 22:1–8). It was not primarily about hygiene, as it would be for us.

On the face of it, extending the law could be understood as a reasonable plea for the priesthood of all believers. Jesus, however, sees in it an illegitimate desire to create new laws that serve only to smother and annul the primary, God-given laws of scripture. When such humanly derived laws become a requirement rather than a personal choice, they can lead to condemnatory attitudes towards those who do not choose to follow them. This is a form of self-righteous legalism, and here is Jesus' bone of contention with the Pharisees. Indeed, sometimes the conflict with scriptural laws was more blatant, as it was with the practice known as 'Corban' mentioned in verse 5 (see also Mark 7:11).

When humanly created traditions trump the word of God, we surely have a serious situation (v. 6). Some careful thought might lead us to the conclusion that the Christian church has plenty of similar traditions. Come to think of it, you might consider that there are a number of ways in which Christians and Pharisees resemble each other. No wonder the church stands in need of being continually reformed according to the word of God.

Jesus proposes his own view in the closing words of this passage. His plea is for inward reality, the worship of the heart and faithfulness to God's authentic word as the true law. In this he is fully in line with what is taught in the Hebrew scriptures, in ways that the Pharisees were not.

2 Religion from the heart

Matthew 15:10–20

This passage continues and underlines Jesus' words in the previous one. Religion is often to do with outward rituals and acts that send out signals of piety to any who are observing, but this is not what Jesus was advocating. The purity practices of Judaism that related to temple worship did not affect most of the people most of the time in their everyday life. However, the Pharisees' extension of these practices was affecting many people for much of the time. Such religious practice was likely to lead to a focus on not infringing the rules, maintaining an outward correctness and purity, and being seen to conform to what was expected. The potential perils of such religion no doubt gave rise to Jesus' harsh accusation of 'hypocrisy' (which appears seven times in Matthew 23 alone). The Pharisees were on the wrong track, acting as blind guides, leading people in the wrong direction (v. 14).

By contrast, Jesus wishes to extend 'purity' in the other direction— inwards, to what takes place in the inner depths of the human heart. We might rightly imagine that there were other Jewish teachers who agreed more with Jesus than with the Pharisees; Jesus was not setting himself against Judaism as such, but against a particular form of Judaism that was gaining ground in his day. At the same time, he was drawing on a strand of Old Testament teaching that claimed, 'The sacrifice acceptable to God is a broken spirit; a broken and contrite heart, O God, you will not despise' (Psalm 51:17).

What spoils human beings is not what goes into us, says Jesus, but what comes out of us—out of our desires, will, motives, dispositions and attitudes. Although this teaching does not abolish food laws and the like, it certainly relativises them, making them less important. The heart is what matters (v. 19). The 'heart' is a reference to the centre of our inner lives, our will and affections. Put these things right and our outward lives become right. True religion, therefore, as distinct from outward form, involves the transformation of the heart, the turning of our inner life towards God so that it might be in alignment with the one who is the source of all goodness and righteousness.

3 Unexpected encounter

Matthew 15:21–28

This encounter with a Canaanite woman is one of the most radical moments in the ministry of Jesus. Jesus is on the coast (v. 21), perhaps taking a pause from ministry in non-Israelite territory. As a Canaanite, the woman is a Gentile and a descendant of one of the tribes the Israelites displaced when they possessed the land under Joshua a thousand years before. Despite this ethnic background, she addresses Jesus as the Jewish Messiah (v. 22). Jesus is reluctant to help (v. 24) and the disciples are keen to be rid of her. She does not fit into Jesus' understanding of his mission, which is, at this point, focused on Israel. But the woman is desperate, direct and bold, and is prepared to answer Jesus back when he meets her with offputting, possibly even offensive words (vv. 26–27). Because of her evident faith, Jesus grants her request and the daughter is healed.

It is a wonderful, compassionate story, but also a radical one. Can it be that in this encounter Jesus actually learns more about himself? Can it be that he is actually taught by a desperate Canaanite woman? His reference to 'the lost sheep of the house of Israel' reflects the typical Jewish nationalism of his day. To be sure, the inclusion of the Gentiles has already been foreshadowed in this Gospel in the adoration of the magi (2:1–12), the impact Jesus has made throughout Syria (4:24) and his encounter with the centurion (8:5–13). But here, with the woman's help, he once more breaks beyond the boundaries of Israel, as surely as he is standing on Gentile ground. Liberation from spiritual oppression and the gift of healing (vv. 22, 28) cannot be confined to Israel but are to be God's gift wherever there are those who call on the name of the Lord with faith.

That Jesus in the course of his earthly life had to learn this through experience; that his knowledge of God and God's purposes needed to unfold over time, just as they do for us; that Jesus was himself a learner of the ways of the Lord, just as we are of the ways of Jesus, is a radical claim. But it is entirely consistent with the fact that he 'emptied himself… humbled himself and became obedient to the point of death' (Philippians 2:7–8).

4 Jesus the wonder worker

Matthew 15:29–39

It is beyond doubt that Jesus worked wonders, but how this was the case is a matter for consideration. Believers in Jesus attribute it, quite understandably, to the power of God at work within him. The reference to a mountain (v. 29) suggests that Jesus was mediating healing grace from God. Sceptics are more inclined to look for psychological or hypnotic factors or to the gullibility of the crowds. They point to people who apparently work wonders in other religious traditions or to illusionists such as Derren Brown who claim to do similar feats through purely naturalistic means. But do showmen or women really heal?

Despite the common claim that reasonable people should 'follow the evidence', it is surprisingly easy to reject the evidence when it conflicts with our prior beliefs. The evidence of the Gospels is that Jesus made a profound and beneficial impact upon people, beyond what is normally possible. The range of healings that Jesus worked is impressively broad (vv. 30–31) and confirms what the Gospel has previously stated in 4:23–25. It takes only a little imagination to recognise the relief from suffering and the gratitude that Jesus brought about. No wonder the people loved him.

They loved him because he so evidently loved them—the poor, helpless and afflicted. In verse 32 Jesus speaks of the compassion he feels for the hungry crowd. He does what he does neither for personal or financial gain nor to boost his popularity, but simply because he feels for people and cares about them. In this he truly expresses the love of God. The God of Israel (v. 31) is a God of steadfast love and compassion. Doing good in his name never needs to be justified.

The feeding of the 4000 follows on from that of the 5000 in 14:13–21, and we might wonder why there need to be two such mighty works.

Because of the common details, some scholars claim that they are different versions of the same event. Perhaps a clue is being given in that the second feeding is placed after an episode in which a Canaanite woman finds faith, and that Jesus is now ministering in an ethnically mixed area. What Jesus has first done for Jewish people, he now does for Gentiles. He feeds them all abundantly with food that comes from God.

5 The sign of Jonah

Matthew 16:1–12

If I were a disciple of Jesus, writing a Gospel about his life and doings, I might be tempted to depict myself and my comrades in a more positive light than the Gospels actually do. Consistently, the disciples come across as dull-witted, slow to get the point and certainly lacking in robust faith (v. 8). They have yet to 'get' Jesus or the meaning of his works, and in that regard this passage prepares us well for the one that is to follow.

Once more, here, Jesus' ministry is being contested by Pharisees and Sadducees. They are looking for a sign. It might occasionally be right to do this if, for instance, we are seeking guidance, but it all depends on the spirit in which we ask. Even if Jesus does give a sign, the likelihood is that these leaders will reject it because they are asking not in a humble spirit of inquiry but in unbelief, determined not to believe, whatever happens. This unhelpful influence is to be guarded against, since it can spread, as yeast does in a loaf (vv. 6, 11). Jesus takes his own advice and declines to throw his pearls before swine (7:6).

All signs require an element of interpretation, and this, in turn, requires a right disposition. But there is one sign that Jesus considers to be decisive, which he calls 'the sign of Jonah' (v. 4). This truly is a 'sign from heaven'—that is, from God (v. 1). The Gospel here repeats what has already been made clear in 12:40: Jonah was three days and nights in the belly of the sea monster; Jesus will be three days and nights in the heart of the earth, and then he will be raised (see Jonah 1:17).

Although the point is clear, the details do not fit perfectly together. Jesus was raised on the third day but was in the grave for only two nights. Perhaps Jesus, at this point, was not entirely sure how the timetable of death and resurrection would work out, only that it would do. Alternatively, perhaps Jesus meant to stress that he would be as dead as it is possible to be, and then would be raised out of death by the power of God. That really would be a sign to be believed.

6 Building on a rock

Matthew 16:13–20

This passage surely counts as the hinge on which the whole of the Gospel turns. The dull-witted disciples at last get the point. Jesus is now in Caesarea Philippi, well to the north and definitely in Gentile territory. He is still educating his disciples, drawing them out by asking probing questions. First he wants to know what the word about him is on the streets; various options are rehearsed. Then follows a hugely momentous question, which lies at the heart of faith: 'But who do you say that I am?' Is there a more important question?

On this occasion Peter is gloriously right. His confession of Jesus hits the jackpot and does so by inspiration and revelation from God (v. 17). Human searching and divine response meet together here. The decisive insight that enables the whole Jesus-enterprise to move to its next stage is realised and Jesus presses its implications with the promise now to build his church (v. 18).

Few passages have been more disputed than this one. The different understandings that have been advanced account for some of the major divergences in Christian churches. For Romans, the rock on which the Church is to be built is Peter himself. After all, he was the most prominent among the disciples and the first to articulate Jesus' true identity, and should be considered to have priority among them. This gives rise to the 'Petrine principle' of having a continual line of successors to Peter, who was believed (at least by some) to have become the bishop of Rome. Reformers disagree. For them, the rock is not Peter but Peter's confession, the insight or doctrine that Jesus is 'the Messiah, the Son of the living God' (v. 16). Peter was just the first to give voice to what we should all believe. For Radicals, the doctrine is certainly important but Peter is not dispensable. Rather, he is a sign of committed and confessing discipleship. The rock on which the Church is built is made up of disciples who confess Jesus and follow him. They hear the words of Jesus and build on them (7:24).

Whichever interpretation fits best, the Caesarea moment is key to the whole of the Gospel and the whole ministry of Jesus. For the first time, the word 'church' appears, with the promise that Christ will build it and bestow his authority upon it.

Guidelines

From our encounters with Jesus in these passages it should be clear that he is not the 'Jesus meek and mild' of religious mythology. The Jesus of the Gospels is righteous, confrontational and fierce. He can dispute with Pharisees and Sadducees. He is tough on his disciples and expects much from them. He can confront evil influences and put them to flight with a word. He can do wonders way beyond human capacities and powers. The life of Jesus was an exposed one, open to others' disagreements and criticisms and constantly vulnerable to attack. All these things become more intense as the Gospel moves on.

Yet beyond all this we see the heart of Jesus—his desire for deeply felt response to God and inner holiness; his compassion and will to heal those who are desperate and afflicted; his urge to feed the hungry, both Jews and Gentiles. If out of the history of Israel and its holy scriptures there arise many humanising and compassionate instincts, most of all from the prophets, we see them coming to some kind of embodiment in Jesus. He is the incarnation of the humane and merciful vision that we find in the law and prophets at their finest. He is the spelling out through the medium of a human life what it means for Christ to be truly the Son of God and for God to be truly Christ-like.

We should consider it amazing that God is spelt out for us in the form of a human life at the centre of the divine purpose. This, surely, is a language we can understand—the supreme cross-cultural communication that comes from heaven to earth, from the divine into the human (John 1:14). In the light of who Jesus was and is, we should ask ourselves: what kind of human being am I called to be? Jesus is rightly understood as the great humaniser, the one who shows us what it means, in a particular place and time in history, to be a human being in the image of God. He therefore enables us to be true human beings, in the image of the one who is himself the image of God's own being (Hebrews 1:3).

1 The revaluation of all values

Matthew 16:21–23

Today's reading is on the short side, but that serves to indicate that its content is to be noted carefully. The sense that we have turned a corner in this Gospel is underlined by the opening words: 'From that time on'.

It seems counterintuitive that the previous, momentous passage should end with Jesus ordering his disciples not to tell anyone what they have just discovered (16:20). We might expect the precise opposite: 'Now that you have understood, tell everyone about it.' Yet Jesus, who never used the word 'Messiah' of himself, is reticent. He is in the process of redefining what the Messiah is. The time is not right for open proclamation. The words of this passage are part of that task. They speak of one who will suffer and be killed and then rise. Some Messiah!

Jesus is now setting his face to go to Jerusalem, knowing that suffering awaits him there (Luke 9:51). However much they have understood, the disciples are still a long way from full understanding. Peter, perhaps buoyed up by having been called 'blessed', even has the temerity to take Jesus on one side and rebuke him. The fall from being so right in one verse to being rebuked as Satan in another is stupendous (vv. 22–23). Of course, he means it well and speaks out of love for Jesus, but in effect he is placing a stumbling-block in Jesus' way, seeking to dissuade him from the difficult road he has to travel and, as in the temptations in Matthew 4, offering him an easier way. Jesus knows that there is no easy option and that a proper understanding of the mind of God requires him to tread the way of the cross.

Once more we note how the Gospel presents the disciples—in this case, even the leader of the disciples—in a very unflattering light. This is surely a sign of authenticity. But who (other than Jesus) can blame Peter for thinking as the rest of us think (v. 23)? Who among us has not had a

'Peter moment' when, having hit the heights, we have immediately failed? Following Jesus means learning to think very differently about life, the universe and everything.

2 Taking up the cross

Matthew 16:24–28

Jesus immediately spells it out. If we are to follow him at all, we are to follow him on the way to the cross. This means an initial act of self-denial by which we yield control of our own lives to him, wherever that may lead, followed by a continual process of walking in Jesus' footsteps and preferring God's will to our own. This feels like death, yet paradoxically it is the way to life. It is hard to explain purely as a mathematical calculation, but it follows a kind of logic which claims that it is no mistake to lose what we cannot keep, to gain what we cannot lose.

The mystery ingredient in the logic is, of course, God. Faith is a risk, a leap of trust, but it is warranted in the light not only of Jesus' teaching but of the God who raised him from the dead. Those who trust in the Lord will not be put to shame. There will be a final reckoning, a vindication of the risk of faith when the 'Son of Man' (Jesus' preferred self-designation) is finally revealed as he is (v. 27). Although presently incognito, the Son of Man will one day come in glory and will put all things right.

When will this be? Words such as those in verse 28 have long been understood as references to the final coming of the Lord, to be expected soon after the words were spoken, but this creates a problem. Jesus apparently expected some of his hearers not to die before it all happened, and here we are 2000 years later. It is more likely, though, that Jesus was referring to his vindication first in the resurrection, then in the ascension, then in the coming of the Spirit at Pentecost. All of these events may be understood as comings of the kingdom of the Son of Man. Others see his further vindication in the fall of Jerusalem in AD70, when his later warnings came to pass (23:34–39).

Jesus' words are capable of multiple fulfilments. In the light of the whole New Testament, however, we may affirm that there is an ultimate and final fulfilment, which we still await but for which the comings of the

Son of Man prepare us, inspiring us with hope. In the risky life of faith in Jesus, that is a destiny for which we can gladly give up everything.

3 Transfigured

Matthew 17:1–8

The author of John's Gospel wrote in his Prologue, 'We have seen his glory, the glory as of a father's only son, full of grace and truth' (1:14). In this scene from Matthew's Gospel, Peter, James and John, the inner circle of Jesus' disciples, did exactly that. In the Bible, mountains are often associated with divine encounters, not least in the case of Moses (Exodus 19:20) and Elijah (1 Kings 19:11), who are mentioned here in verse 3. Jesus communes with God with such intensity that he undergoes a change in appearance, his face shining like the sun (compare Moses in Exodus 34:33–35) and his clothes becoming dazzling white.

This is a powerful image that says much about what Christians believe about their Messiah. In the human Jesus, our mediator, the glory of God comes shining through. As often in the Bible, the bright cloud from which God speaks is a sign of the divine presence (v. 5). Jesus is, by the Father's own testimony, God's beloved Son. No wonder the disciples are filled with awe (v. 6). Such experiences occur rarely, but they do happen. Most of us find it difficult to imagine God, and perhaps this is as it should be, but to think of God as pure and dazzling light surely helps us come close to the truth.

God's Son is accompanied by Moses and Elijah, representing the law and the prophets, of which Jesus the beloved Son is the fulfilment. Is there a hint here that the saints of God, though dead, are alive in God and in communion with the saints on earth? At least we can deduce, once more, that the entire sweep of Old Testament scripture and the whole course of Israel's history have led up to the life of this remarkable human being in whom the presence of God is becoming increasingly visible.

For Jesus, this was no doubt a moment of preparation and strengthening for what he had yet to accomplish in Jerusalem. The divine presence would shortly give way to forsakenness (27:46), and even Jesus needed comfort and reassurance as he anticipated his ordeal. For their part, the disciples who were privileged to witness this event were overwhelmed by it—except, of course, that Peter characteristically had something inept to say (v. 4). He would have done better to hold his tongue and gaze in wonder.

4 The coming of Elijah

Matthew 17:9–13

Once more, Jesus counsels the disciples to be reticent about the powerful vision they have just seen. The 'messianic secret' surfaces again. The work of redefining what it means to be the Messiah must run its course before such a vision can be understood. The appropriate time to speak will be after Jesus has been crucified and has risen. These will be the great redefining moments that will change for ever the disciples' perspectives on God, salvation and messiahship.

Meanwhile, they are full of questions. In the transfiguration, the kingdom of God has drawn very close and Jesus has been shown in their eyes as the one in whom it is fulfilled. He is more than a forerunner of the kingdom; he is the embodiment of the kingdom itself. What, then, of the prophecy in Malachi 4:5: 'Lo, I will send you the prophet Elijah before the great and terrible day of the Lord comes'? How does Elijah fit into God's timetable for the kingdom? The disciples refer to the 'scribes' (v. 10), and it was well established in rabbinic thinking that Elijah would come in connection with the Messiah, although there was no great agreement as to what he would do.

Jesus is clear: the expectation that Elijah would come and restore things was well based and firmly to be believed (v. 11). John the Baptist was Elijah, as the disciples gradually came to see (v. 13)—despite the fact that John himself denied being either the Messiah or Elijah (John 1:21). John clearly did not yet grasp the full significance of his own ministry, but that did not stop him being in God's purpose, more completely than he knew. John was not recognised by those to whom he came, and the work he did was not brought to completeness, but this did not prevent the work of God from going ahead in the ministry of Jesus.

The thought that John's ministry had a greater significance than he himself was able to perceive is an interesting one. John was frail flesh and blood and was eventually done to death. It is doubtful that he ever felt like a hero. Perhaps it is the same with our own fragile attempts to be witnesses to the Christ. By God's grace, we are more significant than we feel.

5 An epileptic boy is healed

Matthew 17:14–20

Meanwhile, at the bottom of the mountain a crowd has gathered and the rest of Jesus' disciples are having a hard time. They cannot heal an epileptic boy of his affliction. Jesus seemingly does not subscribe to the doctrine that 'it's all right to fail'. He is impatient with them and accuses them of being faithless and perverse (v. 17). He is disappointed by their ineptitude. Perhaps it is all right to fail, but sometimes at the other end of our failure is a desperate person, a suffering child or an anguished parent at their wits' end. Being less tolerant of our own failures might help us to help them.

As befits one who is the embodiment of the kingdom of God, Jesus steps in and does what his disciples cannot. He rebukes the demon and the boy is instantly cured. Such is God's power, if we can place ourselves at its service. Of course, this raises questions about what was wrong with the boy in the first place. Was it a case of mental illness, described in the language of the day, or is what we call epilepsy simply the description of a symptom that could have multiple causes? In our mysterious world we would be unwise to close off the category of 'the demonic', even if we don't fully understand what it means.

Diagnosis is not the only challenge here. Jesus indicates that, like him, if we have faith we can move mountains (v. 20). In fact, if we have faith the size of a mustard seed, which is very small, we can do remarkable, even impossible things. It should be said that this verse and others like it have sometimes been used as a pretext for attempting unwise endeavours in the name of the Lord. Is it one of Jesus' occasional moments of hyberbole, though with a serious point to be made? It would be wrong, however, to see this verse, in typical Western fashion, as a problem. Jesus conjoined great faith with profound knowledge of God's will and purpose (see, for example, Mark 11:20–24). It is safe to have outrageous faith when we can be sure it corresponds to God's will. As Jesus is once more acting here with perfect compassion and mercy towards people who are helpless, we can infer that he is indeed acting in harmony with God's will.

6 Predicting the passion

Matthew 17:22–23

Today's reading consists of two solitary and poignant verses. Actually they are not so solitary. Since the Gospel has turned on its hinge with Peter's confession (16:16), Jesus has begun to speak openly and clearly about the fate that awaits him in Jerusalem. These verses are the second, or possibly third, prediction of his passion. We noted the first in 16:21. The present one follows the same order: Jesus will be betrayed; he will be killed; he will be raised. In between, there have been the words in 17:12 about the Son of Man suffering at the hands of those who killed John the Baptist (presumably a general reference to the authorities) and a reference to the fact that he would be raised from the dead (17:9).

Those of a more sceptical disposition find it hard to believe that Jesus could predict his future with such accuracy. They are inclined to believe that Matthew is helping the narrative along by inserting predictions, after the event, into the mouth of Jesus. It is certainly the case that he is arranging his Gospel to best effect, bringing out the full force of the drama as a good writer should, but is it really so incredible that Jesus could not only guess what awaited him but the order in which the events would happen? Human beings do sometimes have premonitions. Jesus was well aware that Jerusalem 'kills the prophets and stones those who are sent to it' (23:37). He has shown himself to be fully aware of what happened to John the Baptist (17:12). It was not beyond him to discern the patterns and deduce what might happen. Moreover, he had communed with Moses and Elijah on the mountain of transfiguration, with whom he had been, in the words of a different Gospel, 'speaking of his departure, which he was about to accomplish at Jerusalem' (Luke 9:31). He knew what awaited him and was resolved to run his course. The disciples were distressed.

Jesus was driven by a sense of necessity. At any moment right up to the end, he could have chosen a different course. On the human level he did not need to suffer and die, but on the level of 'divine things' (16:23) it was required of him, and it was what he required of himself.

Guidelines

A prominent sceptic was asked why he thought Christianity had been so successful. He answered that it was because of two things. First, the Christian religion is very persuasive. It is intellectually powerful and has seized and held human imaginations for centuries. Second, he said, 'it's such a great story'. Some would call it 'the greatest story ever told'. We have to agree on all points. Even if it is not true (which I for one am far from believing), the story of Jesus, related to us through the many stories contained in our Gospels, is deeply moving, full of surprises and simply astonishing. For all that has been written about Jesus in the discipline known as 'Jesus Studies', and for all the propositions and proposals that have been advanced as keys to and insights into his ministry, we have yet to do justice to the sheer mystery of his person. Either the Gospel writers (whose identity we do not know for sure, since none of them name themselves—the Gospels have been given names by tradition) were total geniuses in inventing the portraits that they painted, or their subject, Jesus himself, was everything they claimed he was, and more besides.

Without the Gospels we would know little about the actual life and ministry of Jesus, and little about the world he inhabited. Much of what we know of first-century Judaism is gleaned from the Gospels. The rest of the New Testament is testimony to the life- and history-changing impact that Jesus made. When we consider that he came from peasant stock and was a working carpenter without formal education (although the education he did have was advanced for its day), that he lived for no more than 33 years, and that he died a shameful and undeserved death as both a blasphemer and a political insurrectionist, we must surely be in awe.

Purely on the human level, Jesus excites our admiration. If I were an unbeliever I would still have to love Jesus for the sheer quality of his humanity. But it is through his humanity that something more shines— the beauty, vitality and glory of the living God in whom Jesus believed and from whom he came.

1 In the fish's mouth

Matthew 17:24–27

In Jesus' day, Jewish males over the age of 20 across the world were required to pay a temple tax, a coin that went towards the maintenance of the temple in Jerusalem. It is not surprising that this was resented, either for reasons of sheer meanness or because of conscientious objections to what the temple had become—a 'den of robbers' (21:13). Jesus shared these reservations and, as we shall see, was later to express his objection in no uncertain terms. But the time for that was not quite right, and when the tax collectors came calling (suspecting that Jesus was reluctant to pay), Jesus played for time. As a Son of the king of the universe, Jesus believed himself to be a free man, above such obligations (v. 26). Sometimes, however, the wise thing is not to insist on our rights and freedoms, especially if it might lead to distracting conflicts (v. 27).

What follows is so strange that some commentators think that a parable has been transformed into an actual incident. As his parables are often enigmatic, so is this instruction. Jesus tells Simon Peter to go and catch a fish (they are still in Capernaum, where both Peter and Jesus are at home: v. 24). The first one he hooks will have a coin in its mouth with which he can pay the tax for both of them. Now, although Jesus says this, we are not told that Peter did as he was told or what resulted. Perhaps, indeed, it was just a way of telling Peter to catch a fish, sell it and pay.

Jesus is steering a course between obediently paying the tax as required and refusing payment altogether—making payment in such a dismissive way as not to imply endorsement of the temple racket. As he once counselled his disciples, he is being as wise as a serpent and as innocent as a dove (10:16). This is the kind of wisdom that Christians today should pray to inherit, since we too live in a world with many aspects that we might choose not to endorse. Yet to be overly sensitive in the small things might mean that we lessen our ability to stand against the bigger evils when they confront us.

2 The humility of a child

This particular incident is sparked by the disciples' question about greatness. Similar moments are recorded at various points in the Gospels, and the question might be described as a preoccupation with rank: who ranks higher than whom in the kingdom of God? There is a characteristically human dynamic here, since, consciously or otherwise, we do have a tendency to look for a 'pecking order' in our social relations. Equally, as organisations and institutions develop, ranks of pre-eminence and prestige tend to emerge. Perhaps this is inevitable; perhaps also it is beneficial, as a way of allocating responsibilities according to 'pay grade'. Whichever way we see it, these ranks conflict with the ways of the kingdom if they lack the powerful ingredients of humility and mutual service.

For Jesus, the model recipient of the kingdom of heaven is a child. His focus is not so much on the presumed innocence of a child (as we all know, children are not always models of kindness) as on a child's humility and lack of status. People who are proud and think themselves clever do not represent the kingdom well, if at all. The disciples of Jesus were relatively uneducated and disadvantaged by comparison with the more academic culture of synagogue Judaism, but this did not render them less valuable to the kingdom. Nor did it render them incapable of competition or self-importance. Turning away from these attitudes and assuming a humble place before God and others is of the essence of life in the kingdom that Jesus brought. Once more, we find here the revaluation of all values that took place through Jesus. What some consider greatness is nothing of the sort for him; what some consider insignificance and lack of importance is exactly what Jesus values (v. 4).

We may also note here the love and respect that Jesus had for children, a characteristic that emerges throughout his ministry (see, for example, Mark 10:13–16) and will be re-emphasised in the following verses of chapter 18. There is great tenderness in his words and actions, and, if we do indeed believe that the Father is revealed in the Son, we must follow them through. In the love that God has for all he has made, there is a tender love for the young and dependent that accords them a special place in the community of the kingdom.

3 Taking radical action

Matthew 18:6–9

If we wish for evidence that Jesus could be as stringent as any Old Testament prophet in his preaching, we need look no further than these verses. Jesus has previously said a fair amount about Gehenna (v. 9), the fiery rubbish tip of final judgement: see Matthew 5:27–30. Verses 8–9 repeat some of that material. If there is something in us that causes us to sin, then swift and radical action needs to be taken.

We can say with confidence that this is one of those biblical passages that deserve to be taken very seriously but not literally. Jesus was a master of hyperbole. We will badly misunderstand scripture if we insist on always taking it literally. It is surely not Jesus' intention that the community of his disciples should be blind and without hands, as most of us would be, on a literal reading of this passage. Self-mutilation was not his intention, but radical action is. We should not be soft on ourselves, tolerating our sins as if they were no kind of problem to God or ourselves. If they are not dealt with, they will destroy us, as surely as will the fires of Gehenna, says Jesus. The doctrines of forgiveness and justification by faith are not to be used as excuses for sin. They call us rather to 'die to sins and live for righteousness' (1 Peter 2:24, NIV). One such sin is the competitive spirit that his disciples reveal in verse 1.

Jesus' stern words directed at our tolerance of our own sins are paralleled by equally stern warnings against putting 'stumbling blocks' in the way of 'little ones' (vv. 6–7). The immediate context suggests child protection: it is a terrible thing to cause a young life to stumble or fall. The community of Jesus' followers should be the safest of spaces in which the young might be nurtured and formed. But the 'little ones' might also refer to the disciples themselves, those who believe in Jesus and are seeking to follow him. In this case, 'stumbling blocks' might refer to false or distorted teaching that deviates from Christ's way. To cause any of the disciples to stumble or fall, whether the stumbling block comes from within or outside their own community, is a heinous crime, worthy of severe judgement. A two-ton millstone is not to be trifled with (v. 6).

4 Angels and vulnerability

Matthew 18:10–14

The chapter continues with the theme of 'little ones', and we have to take a view, preferably an inclusive one, as to who they are. They could be children, as suggested by 18:2, or they could be vulnerable disciples, as might be suggested by the parable that follows in verses 12–14. They might equally be anybody who is at risk on the margins of society, such as the 'widows and orphans' so frequently mentioned in the Hebrew scriptures. Perhaps all these categories are intended, and the point is that although all or any of them might be 'despised' in society at large (v. 10), with God they enjoy a special kind of protection. Once more we are called to a revaluation of our values, to think as God thinks rather than as humans do.

The angels mentioned in verse 10 need not be understood as personal guardian angels so much as the angels of the Lord that collectively 'encamp around those who fear him' (Psalms 34:7, 91:11). The fact that they do not veil their faces when they look continually on God (in contrast to the seraphim in Isaiah 6:2) suggests that they have a special place before God, as do those they guard. Here is God's tender love for those who are at risk.

Such love is amplified in the parable of the lost sheep, in which it is emphasised three times that the sheep has 'gone astray' (vv. 12–13). The shepherd does not shrug his (or her) shoulders and say, 'Ninety-nine out of 100 isn't too bad.' Rather, a loving shepherd (and, we are tempted to say, a daring one) puts the 99 at risk for the sake of the one that is lost, and rejoices over it more than over those that are safe (v. 13). Through the hyperbole, we can grasp that such is the tender love of God and of his beloved Son (17:5), bordering on the daring in the risks it takes to find those who are lost.

Surely this must say something to us about our willingness to move beyond the safe, comfortable conditions in which most of us live, to do something risky for the children, the vulnerable, the lost and those one-time disciples who have gone astray. Discipleship is about Spirit-inspired imitation of God's own Son and God's own self.

5 Discipling one another

Matthew 18:15–20

There are only three occasions in all the Gospels when the word 'church' appears on the lips of Jesus. We encountered the first in his great promise to Peter (16:18). Now we meet the other two in verse 17. (Some gender-inclusive Bible versions also change the word 'brother' or 'brother and sister' in verse 15 to 'church member', but this is not original.) Some scholars argue that Jesus never intended to found a church anyway, and they are probably right if they mean any of the powerful institutions that go by that name today. But Jesus certainly intended to gather a community around himself, seeing it as the beginning of a wider community that would follow on.

The defining characteristic of that community is given in verse 20: the Christian community exists wherever there are those who gather in Christ's name and he is in the midst. Here he speaks of himself as the risen Christ, spiritually present in the community. This is the simplest and most important definition of the church that we might think of. It doesn't take many people to be a church. Jesus specifies two or three men or women, in contrast to the ten males required to form a synagogue. Given that Jesus was used to attracting large crowds, however, we might suspect that he had larger communities in mind.

Because Christ will be in the midst of his church as it gathers, that community will be empowered by the life and Spirit of Christ. This will enable it to pray effectively and well (v. 19). The church has genuine spiritual authority in the presence of God to decide and to act (v. 18). Moreover, believers have a responsibility to keep one another up to the mark, to disciple each other when they go astray (following on from the parable of the lost sheep).

Church discipline is never a popular subject or task, but Jesus sets out a process in verses 15–17. We must see this process not as punishment but as a form of pastoral mediation, a non-aggressive attempt to hold one another to the way of Christ. If the final step in the process (and it is a very final step) involves treating one who has strayed as 'a pagan or a tax collector' (NIV), we should remember that Jesus was known precisely as a 'friend of tax collectors and sinners' (Luke 7:34).

6 Questions of forgiveness

This full-length parable, prompted by a question from Peter, is typical of Jesus. Rabbinic sources counselled forgiving an offender three times, so Peter is being expansive in wondering whether seven times is enough. It's nowhere near enough for Jesus, however, for whom 77 times (or even 70 times seven—the translation can go either way) is closer to the mark. But who's counting? 'Doing the maths' is not the point, because the point goes beyond calculation.

Those who have been forgiven also need to forgive: 'And forgive us our debts, as we also have forgiven our debtors' (6:12). This is a basic law of the spiritual life, and it is pointed up in the parable that Jesus relates. A 'slave' or servant is pardoned a debt amounting to millions of pounds (v. 24), but, on leaving his king's presence, he encounters a fellow servant who owes him a few hundred (v. 28). He seizes the fellow servant by the throat and nearly chokes him. The dissonance is astonishing. Having fallen on his knees before his king and received not just a debt-holiday but total forgiveness, he cannot find it in his own heart to have mercy on a comrade. This is both wrong and shameful, as is plain for all to see (v. 31). He deserves his fate and the king acts in a righteous way by revoking his forgiveness (v. 34).

Jesus often told parables that leave us wondering. It is not difficult to get the main point here, but is it helpful to have a reference to the torturer in verse 34, and are we not troubled by the analogy drawn with the heavenly Father in verse 35? To a certain extent, this language is cartoon-like and not to be pressed to the limit. Yet, as the parables were fashioned both to provoke and to irritate deadened consciences, so they are meant to shock us too into a recognition of reality. Failure to forgive is a serious business when all of us exist solely on the ground of having been forgiven. As the Israelites were frequently enjoined to have mercy on the aliens and the oppressed precisely because they themselves had once been oppressed slaves in Egypt (Deuteronomy 15:15), so the follower of Jesus must remember that he or she exists by divine forgiveness alone. Forgiveness is not just an act; it is a way of life.

Guidelines

The way of the world tells us to get our retaliation in first. Unfortunately, such ways lead only to a vicious cycle of destruction. The way of forgiveness tells us to let go, and not to let 'roots of bitterness' spring up within or between us (Hebrews 12:15). Yet how easy or desirable or even moral is this?

We may have seen Christians who have been grievously and tragically wronged quickly appearing in the media to declare their forgiveness of the wrongdoers. This is magnificent, a remarkable testimony, and we wonder how readily non-Christians could do the same. It is certainly better than being for ever eaten up by bitterness: that would indeed be torture, even a form of Gehenna. Yet forgiveness for truly evil acts, as distinct from momentary slights, can never be easy. When God works forgiveness in human hearts, it involves the cost and pain of the cross. When we forgive, it can only be after having truly felt the pain of what has been done to us or taken from us. Forgiveness is, after all, a journey rather than a momentary pronouncement.

When people do grievous evil, we should be careful not to gloss over that evil as if it did not matter. Forgiveness is free but it is not cheap. The horror of the wrongdoing needs to be faced by both forgiver and forgiven alike. Many offences can be dismissed as insignificant, and we do well not to take offence easily, but some offences against the person or church or community should surely not be forgiven easily or until the depth of the wrong has been properly recognised.

Luke's record of the conversation expresses it slightly differently. There, Jesus says, 'And if the same person sins against you seven times a day, and turns back to you seven times and says, "I repent," you must forgive' (Luke 17:4). Can there properly be forgiveness without prior repentance? Whereas the will to forgive should always be in our hearts, for forgiveness to flow the request for forgiveness needs to be made. When this happens, it is a hard heart indeed that can refuse.

FURTHER READING

Matthew Black and H.H. Rowley, *Peake's Commentary on the Bible*, Thomas Nelson, 1963

Amy-Jill Levine and Marc Zvi Brettler, *The Jewish Annotated New Testament*, Oxford University Press, 2011

Leon Morris, *The Gospel According to Matthew*, IVP, 1992

Tom Wright, *Matthew for Everyone Part 1 (Chapters 1—15)* and *Part 2 (Chapters 16—28)*, SPCK, 2002

The Psalter and the Celtic saints

The early Celtic church had a high regard for scripture, and the Celts particularly loved the book of Psalms. In monastic communities, psalms were used as a tool for the teaching of literacy and for acts of devotion, not only at the monastic offices but at many other times—including, it is said, while doing ablutions. Celtic Christians would have known them all by heart. I have therefore chosen some passages from the Psalms and three outstanding Celtic saints who help us to explore what encouragement these scriptures may give us in our own life of faith.

The saints concerned were all intimately part of the monastic communities to which they belonged, and were very much in touch with the wider communities that they served. We focus on Patrick of Irish fame, David (known in Wales as Dewi) and, finally, Columba, most famous for his association with Iona. Together they represent different parts of the Celtic church, although, at a time when the sea was the main highway, there was much interchange between these areas, as is illustrated by Columba's story.

Celtic Christians had a number of specific forms of prayer, including prayers connected with honouring the Trinity, connecting with nature, pilgrimage, confession and protection against evil. Patrick especially is associated with the lorica, or 'breastplate prayer', and it is with Patrick that we shall start.

My main source of information on Patrick is his own *Confessio* (c. AD450); on David, the eleventh-century 'Life' written by Rhygyfarch; and on Columba, the seventh-century 'Life' by Adomnan of Iona.

Biblical quotations are taken from the New International Version.

27 February–5 March

1 Patrick waits for salvation

Psalms 13 and 16

Psalm 13 begins, 'How long, Lord? Will you forget me for ever? How long will you hide your face from me? How long must I wrestle with my thoughts?' The story of Patrick begins with a teenager who—like David, to whom this psalm is attributed—knew he was in deep trouble. In Patrick's case, it was because he had been kidnapped when he was 16 and taken from his home (probably in Britain) to Ireland. There he decided 'to turn to God with all my heart', learning to trust in God and find security in him, even in a place of captivity (13:5; 16:5).

While he was out shepherding, like David, Patrick learnt to pray day and night (16:7), and this developed his spiritual understanding. One day he heard a voice saying, 'Behold! Your ship is prepared.' He escaped his captors, travelled 200 miles to a port, and arrived just in time to discover a boat about to leave. The pagan crew were reluctant to take him with them but, after Patrick had prayed, agreed to do so. So far, so good; God had not abandoned him (16:8–10).

Three days later, the boat came to shore at an unknown location and the party began to make their way through a wilderness. However, after 28 days, they had begun to starve and the ship's crew challenged Patrick, as a Christian, to pray for them. He did so and a herd of swine turned up; this was followed by the provision of more food and a dry shelter. Again Patrick was a virtual captive, but God promised him that this situation would continue for only two months. Eventually, after some years, he reached his home and family in Britain.

David spent a long time in the desert in close proximity to those who wished him evil, and whose traps he had to avoid (1 Samuel 22—26). It must have been a lean lifestyle for him too.

David's words towards the end of Psalm 16 must have resonated with Patrick's experience: both could say, 'You make known to me the path of life; you will fill me with joy in your presence' (v. 11), because both had known the presence of God in adversity. In the midst of all their troubles, they were confident in God: 'My heart is glad and my tongue rejoices; my body also will rest secure' (v. 9).

2 Patrick and the shield of faith

Psalm 3

A few years later, to his family's horror, Patrick had a vision asking him to return to Ireland. There, he had a deep spiritual experience, which he felt as an awareness of 'someone praying in him'. This reminded him of Paul's experience described in Romans 8:26, where the apostle, talking about prayer, says, 'The Spirit himself intercedes for us through wordless groans.' Patrick's growth in spiritual understanding was often challenged by friends and foes alike, but this experience served to strengthen him.

The psalmist encountered attacks from many foes, all confident that 'God will not deliver him' (v. 2). Patrick, too, was strongly aware of his need for protection against physical attack and evil spiritual powers, and is famous for the prayer known as 'St Patrick's Breastplate'. This is an example of a 'lorica' prayer for protection against evil. Patrick invokes the mighty power of the Trinity before declaring, 'I arise today, through the strength of Christ's birth and his baptism, his crucifixion and burial, his resurrection and ascension, his descent for the judgement of doom... I summon today all these powers between me and evil... against false prophets, heretics, idolatry... against all that corrupts man's body and soul. Christ shield me today.'

Patrick had to learn to use the shield of faith round about him, remaining confident in God's protection, just as the psalmist did (v. 3; see also Proverbs 2:7–8; Ephesians 6:16). His faith and confidence were answered (v. 4): his most famous victory in Christ was probably the defeat of evil powers on the Hill of Tara, the seat of the high king of Ireland and an important pagan stronghold, after which the church in Ireland began to flourish.

The psalmist calls on God, saying, 'Arise, Lord! Deliver me, my God! Strike all my enemies on the jaw; break the teeth of the wicked' (v. 7). God did this for David and for Patrick, who both knew the reality of spiritual warfare. The same shield of faith is available to us today.

3 St David the water drinker

Psalm 1

Psalm 1 paints a picture of a person who delights in God and is like 'a tree planted by streams of water, which yields its fruit in season' (v. 3). The roots take up the water necessary for fruit to be produced. This could well be said of St David, known in his native Wales as Dewi Sant.

David was born in about AD500. His mother is said to have given birth on a clifftop during a violent thunderstorm, and the rainy weather protected him from attack by a local ruler who saw him as a potential rival. He is credited with a number of miracles, starting with the healing of his schoolmaster from blindness. Later, he was asked to pray for a better water supply, after which a spring appeared, of the sweetest water ever tasted there. As a monk, he would drink only water, earning himself the nickname 'Dewi Dwr', 'Dewi the water drinker'. He was also known for his abstinence from most foods, his great interest in the growing of herbs and his enthusiasm for hard farm labour, rejecting the use of animals for ploughing.

The Celts believed that wet places were sacred places, offering access to the 'other world'. The early saints, including David and his followers, would stand in deep water for long periods of time, holding their arms out in a cross shape while focusing on prayer. This is a sign that they took prayer very seriously, in stark contrast to those whom the psalmist describes, who 'sit in the company of mockers' (v. 1). Just as in the psalmist's time, and in Dewi's too, there are still those who sit and mock, or 'stand in the way that sinners take'.

'Blessed is the one who does not walk in step with the wicked,' says verse 1. During David's time, the Pelagian heresy was growing in influence (that is, the teaching that human beings are not affected by original sin and can therefore choose between good and evil without the grace of God). A general synod of all the bishops of Britain was called, and David participated. It is said that as he spoke to a large crowd, the land rose up under him to form a small hill. This meant that everyone could hear his arguments against the heresy 'ringing out like a trumpet'. The heresy was quashed—'like chaff that the wind blows away' (v. 4).

4 Lift up your hands in the sanctuary

Psalm 134

David founded twelve monasteries in Wales and the south-west of England, so he would have known all about lifting hands in the sanctuary (v. 2). Serious and costly prayer was a key element in the monastic lifestyle. Rhygyfarch, in his *Life of St David*, tells us that 'at sunset they sang psalms with unity of heart on bended knees until the appearance of the stars in the heavens'. This would have been a regular pattern of prayer, following the psalmist's urging: 'Praise the Lord, all you servants of the Lord who minister by night in the house of the Lord' (v. 1). The self-discipline that David showed revealed his attitude to Christian living, intertwined with praise and worship.

David did not put up with mockers or idle people, or with monks who, perhaps unthinkingly, claimed anything as their own possession. David and his monks were hard workers, but, in spite of this lifestyle, tough even by the standards of his time, his monastic movement grew and grew: 'Everywhere voices were raised to heaven in prayer, [people] were brought back to the bosom of the church and offerings of charity distributed to the needy with an open hand.'

Knowing that his life was coming to an end, David spent long hours preaching. On Sunday 1 March, after celebrating the Eucharist, he became very ill and died. His life is summed up well in his dying words: he told his followers to 'keep the faith, and do the little things well'. Psalm 134 is headed 'A song of ascents', reminding us of a journey to the holy place—even the journey through death to meet 'the Maker of heaven and earth' (v. 3).

Our patterns of prayer may not be those of the psalmist or of Dewi Sant, but prayer, praise to God, and the lifting of holy hands in the sanctuary are essential for us too, so that 'the Lord [may] bless you from Zion' (v. 3).

5 Columba's pilgrimage

Psalm 130

Pilgrimage was an essential feature of the Celtic church, and Celtic Christians travelled throughout the known world. In these last two studies we will look at two more of the 'songs of ascent'—psalms thought to have been originally written for use by pilgrims to Jerusalem.

Columba, also known as Columcille, was born in Donegal in December AD521. He founded several monasteries but got into serious trouble when he made a copy of a psalter belonging to St Finnian, without permission. His penalty was to be set adrift in a coracle without an oar, leaving God to decide what would happen next. Thus, in 563, Columba and twelve companions left Ireland in their coracle and sailed to an island, far enough away that they could not see their homeland.

Maybe the little group chose a psalm or two to pray in the midst of their calamity, wondering where the sea would take them and whether they would even survive. Psalm 130 would certainly have been appropriate, beginning, 'Out of the depths I cry to you, Lord… Let your ears be attentive to my cry for mercy' (vv. 1–2). They could have drifted far out into the Atlantic and perished there, but God planned to bring good out of this potential disaster.

The psalmist, although in awe of God, was confident of receiving his forgiveness (vv. 3–4). I imagine that Columba would have felt similar emotions, putting his hope in God's word and waiting for the outcome (v. 5). Drifting on the ocean in the darkness of night would have been the hardest thing about the voyage. The psalmist expresses this sort of anxiety well in verse 6, repeating the phrase 'more than watchmen wait for the morning' to emphasise its importance. Sentries on a city wall, as well as sailors on the ocean, would have understood the feeling well.

Like the psalmist, Columba was to find that 'with [the Lord] is full redemption' (v. 7). The island where his coracle came to shore was Iona. It was there that Columba established his most famous monastery and where the Book of Kells, now regarded as one of the greatest treasures of the Celtic era, was probably produced. Paul wrote to the Roman Christians, 'In all things God works for the good of those who love him' (Romans 8:28), and so it proved for Columba.

6 They will not be put to shame

Psalm 127

Put in a positive light, Columba's voyage was a pilgrimage. An event that could have been a disaster led to the establishment of a very influential monastic community, whose legacy continues to be developed on the same island in our own day.

Columba's pilgrimage can also be seen in terms of the different concepts of 'martyrdom' that the Celtic Christians held. 'White' martyrdom was about making a very serious commitment to following Christ, but without travelling elsewhere. 'Green', much favoured especially by the Irish monks, was about leaving all that was familiar to go on a journey without a particular destination in mind and without necessarily intending to come back, while waiting to see what God did. Columba's adventures were an example of green martyrdom, as were the European travels of the monk Columbanus. ('Red' martyrdom was, of course, the suffering of death for Christ's sake while preaching the gospel.)

As Psalm 127 says, however, 'unless the Lord builds the house' and 'unless the Lord watches over the city', our efforts are all in vain (v. 1). Therefore, the decision to take such a course of action had to be preceded by a call from God and usually had to be verified by the pilgrim's monastery. The psalmist assesses God's blessing in terms of 'children', and a large number of them—a 'quiver... full' (v. 5). Columba certainly had plenty of monastic 'sons', including St Aidan, a monk of Iona who took the gospel east to Northumbria, extending Columba's influence as far as Lindisfarne. The blessing was to continue: Columba's life was recorded by the monk Adomnan about 100 years after his death and, as I have mentioned, Iona is a centre of Christian pilgrimage to this day.

Four years before his death in 597, Columba's strength began to fail but he continued to transcribe books with great skill. Like Dewi, Columba died in his church, just before the community were to say Matins. The rhythm of prayer and praise was ever present in his life. As the psalmist said, those who are blessed by God 'will not be put to shame' (v. 5). As we tread our own pilgrimage path, may that be said of us too.

Guidelines

Here are a few questions and challenges that our engagement with these Celtic saints brings to us.

- How are the themes of heresy and spiritual warfare still relevant to us today?
- How can we, as St David exhorts us, 'keep the faith and do the little things well'?

- What approaches to prayer does the Celtic church encourage us to adopt?
- Self-discipline was a key element in the faithful monastic life. In what ways might we learn from this?
- Do we trust God to bring blessing out of seeming calamity in our lives?

FURTHER READING

Elizabeth Culling, *What is Celtic Christianity?*, Grove, 2008.

Oliver Davies, *Celtic Spirituality*, Paulist Press, 1999.

Calvin Miller, *The Path of Celtic Prayer*, BRF, 2008.

Don't forget to renew your annual
subscription to *Guidelines*!

If you enjoy the notes, why not also
consider giving a gift subscription
to a friend or member of your family?

You will find subscription order forms on pages 156 and 157.

Guidelines is also available from your local Christian bookshop.

Joshua

Joshua recounts events during a key period in the history of the Israelites—the conquest of Canaan and the division of the land between the twelve tribes. It was a time of great social transition as the people settled for the first time in a generation. It was also a time of spiritual challenge. Would the God who had been so relevant in the deserts of Sinai be equally relevant in Canaan, or would the gods of the land prove more attractive? How would these previously nomadic people adapt their customs and beliefs to a new situation? The future religious life of Israel would be shaped by these questions.

Joshua has been at once an inspiration and a challenge to Christians through the ages. Verses such as 'Choose for yourselves this day whom you will serve... but as for me and my household, we will serve the Lord' (24:15) and 'This book of the Law shall not depart out of your mouth; you shall meditate on it day and night... Do not be frightened or dismayed, for the Lord your God is with you wherever you go' (1:8–9) have spoken powerfully to people. This was never more evident than in the yearnings of the slaves in the American deep south, who hoped that one day they too would 'cross the Jordan' into the promised land and see the walls of their oppression, like the walls of Jericho, 'come tumbling down'.

Yet we live in an age when we are acutely aware of genocide, atrocity and conflict, regarding them as anathema to the gospel of love and to God as revealed in Christ. Thus, the mission of the Israelites in Joshua to displace or kill existing populations and occupy a land already inhabited is profoundly disturbing. This recurring theme of *herem* (meaning 'devote' or 'destroy') has always been a theological difficulty for Christians. Origen, in the third century AD, interpreted Joshua allegorically; Calvin saw *herem* as the justified reaction of a righteous God to the sin of humankind, necessary to preserve the holiness of Israel. Contemporary writers such as Christopher Hitchens and Richard Dawkins often point to the book of Joshua as evidence of the genocidal nature of God.

Today, most Christian commentators live with an uneasy tension between the God of Joshua and the God of the New Testament and recognise that Joshua is a product of its age. In our readings we will look at a couple of approaches that modern theologians have taken to *herem*.

Biblical quotations are from the NRSV unless otherwise indicated.

1 Introducing Joshua the leader

Numbers 27:12–21

The greatest leaders are grown, not suddenly picked out of nowhere, and Joshua was no exception. He did not appear on the scene spontaneously, just as Moses died. Reading the account of the Israelites during the exodus, we see how he and other potential leaders were nurtured during Moses' tenure. Joshua was Moses' right-hand man for 40 years, living in the tent where people went to inquire of God (Exodus 33:11). He was with Moses when he went up Mount Sinai to receive the ten commandments (Exodus 24:13) and was one of those chosen to spy out the land of Canaan in Numbers 13. Tellingly, Moses changed his name from Hoshea ('salvation') to Joshua ('the Lord saves') by appending the Lord's name to his (Numbers 13:16). Often in the Bible, a change of name denotes a special purpose or destiny; thus Moses marked him out as 'someone to watch'. As well as being a religious leader, Joshua was a military commander, leading the armies of Israel to success against the Amalekites (Exodus 17:8–13). So, when Moses reached the end of his life, Joshua was the obvious choice to succeed him.

Our reading today describes the moment when all this potential and training bore fruit, with a partial transfer of authority. Moses was concerned that the people would be 'like sheep without a shepherd' (v. 17), and asked God to choose the leader to succeed him. Joshua was perhaps the obvious choice, but he was selected primarily because he had 'the spirit of leadership' (v. 18, NIV). Then two important things happened. First, Joshua was affirmed before the whole assembly; second, Moses gave Joshua some of his authority (v. 20). Joshua was, like the best leaders, prepared by his mentor, affirmed publicly, recognised as having the right gifts and, crucially, given as much authority as he could handle at that moment.

Also worthy of note is the involvement of Eleazar in the commissioning and in Joshua's future leadership (vv. 19, 21). Eleazar was the son of Aaron and his successor as high priest. Perhaps there is a hint here that Joshua was Moses' successor but not his equal. Moses had spoken with

God face to face (Exodus 33:11), whereas Joshua would consult with God through the high priest's casting of lots.

2 Be strong and very courageous

Joshua 1

Joshua 1 acts as an abstract of the whole book, summarising the events that will unfold in the coming chapters. The boundaries of the area to be conquered are given in verse 4. Later in the chapter we are reminded that the land given to the tribes of Reuben and Gad and the half-tribe of Manasseh lies in the Transjordan area, east of the River Jordan, so only their fighting men will cross the river to help with the conquest (v. 14).

The main focus of the chapter, however, is God's confirmation of Joshua as leader after Moses' death and the affirmation of this leadership by the Israelites. Continuity from Moses is emphasised. In verses 3, 5 and 7 we are reminded that God promised the land to Moses, that God was with Moses and that Joshua is to follow Moses' instructions. In the rest of the book, the continuity from Moses to Joshua is subtly reinforced. For example, both men lead the Israelites across a body of water to dry land (Exodus 14:21–29; Joshua 3:7–17), both allocate land to the Israelites (Numbers 32; Joshua 13—21), both send out spies (Numbers 13; Joshua 2) and both give lengthy farewell speeches (Deuteronomy 31—33; Joshua 23–24).

Notably and repeatedly, Joshua is reminded to be 'strong and courageous' by both God and the people. Is this, as many commentators claim, a sign that Joshua's courage needed bolstering at this crucial moment? Perhaps. It is difficult to come out of the shadow of a great leader, and the Israelites were facing a daunting task ahead of them. It is one thing to be the deputy, another to have command. Pope John XXIII once said, 'It often happens that I wake up at night and begin to think about the serious problems afflicting the world, and I tell myself, I must talk to the pope about it. Then the next day when I wake up I remember that I am the pope!' But perhaps in Joshua's case commentators have judged him too harshly. As a military leader, the main quality required of him would be courage. It is possible that the many reminders are simply a recognition of this need, and the repetition either emphasises the point or gives a comedic moment as the people unconsciously echo God's words earlier in the chapter (vv. 6, 9, 18).

3 Stones of remembrance

Joshua 4

The Judeo-Christian religious tradition is primarily a historical one. It is anchored not in abstract theories about the character of God but in the remembrance of events that reveal his character. As Rabbi Yisroel ben Eliezer, the founder of Hasidic Judaism, said, 'Forgetfulness leads to exile, while remembrance is the secret of redemption.'

As the Israelites crossed the Jordan into Canaan and a new way of life, the danger was that the oral tradition of the exodus would be lost and forgotten. As a reminder, Joshua ordered twelve of the men crossing the Jordan to pick up a stone with which to make a cairn at Gilgal, to mark the place of the crossing (v. 20). A second cairn was erected in the middle of the river where the priests had stood as the people crossed (v. 9).

The purpose of the cairn in the middle of the river is not entirely clear. If it was visible above the waterline, it might, with the other cairn, have served to mark the route of the crossing. It might also have served to mark a site made holy by the presence of the priests and the ark of the covenant. It is also possible that we have a textual misreading here: it may be that the Israelites placed stones not 'in the midst' (Hebrew *bethoch*) of the river, but 'from the midst' of it (Hebrew *mithoch*), which would mean that only one cairn was present. This is a tempting theory; however, it has no support in the source manuscripts.

The purpose of the cairn erected at Gilgal is obvious and is stated in the text: it will be a memorial (v. 7; Hebrew *zikaron*), reminding future generations of the crossing of the Jordan and marking the spot where it took place (vv. 20–22). For Christians, this finds echoes in the New Testament. In 1 Peter 2:4–5, Jesus is called 'a living stone' in whom we are being built up. In Ephesians 2:19–22 Christ is the cornerstone, and around him are the apostles and prophets. Jesus said, 'Whoever has seen me has seen the Father' (John 14:9). In short, Jesus is our *zikaron*.

4 The walls of Jericho

Joshua 6

It is easy to trace on a map the route taken by the Israelite army as they swept through Canaan. After circumcising all the men who had been born since the exodus and celebrating the Passover (5:2–12), Joshua led the army west from Gilgal, then across the plains to the south (Joshua 6—10). Then they moved north to subdue the more mountainous northern territories, ending at Hazor with the defeat of a coalition of northern kings (ch. 11). Before this campaign could take place, though, the Israelites faced the great walled cities of Jericho and Ai.

Jericho was the first real test they had faced after crossing the River Jordan. The story of Joshua and the battle of Jericho is one of the best-known in the Bible, and it introduces one of the major themes in the book of Joshua: when the Israelites depend on God, they prosper; when they try to be self-reliant, failure follows.

The way the story is told emphasises that this is a divine campaign rather than a military one. The strategy is delivered by God, perhaps through the 'commander of the army of the Lord' who has just encountered Joshua (5:13–15). The instructions make no military sense but are rich in religious symbolism. As they circle the city, the priests are to blow the shofar, or ram's horn. In the Old Testament, the shofar was sounded at key moments of God's presence—for example, when Moses met God at Mount Sinai (Exodus 19:16, 19; 20:18) and when Solomon's temple was dedicated (2 Chronicles 5:13). The presence of the ark of the covenant likewise reminds us of the presence of God among the Israelite army.

It is in the conquest of Jericho that we first see the application of *herem*—the total annihilation of the local population (6:17). What can we make of this? One possibility, outlined by Stern in *The Biblical Herem*, is that the conquest of Canaan is seen in terms of the creation, bringing order out of chaos. Thus, the six days of marching mirror the six days of creation, with the seventh day bringing completeness to the process (in the Bible, the number seven often represents completeness). According to this reading, *herem* is part of the creation process, ushering in the promised kingdom.

5 A small sin with a huge consequence

Joshua 7

In Joshua 7 the theme of obedience and disobedience is graphically displayed. Buoyed by the victory over Jericho, the Israelites forget the admonition of God to 'be careful to obey' (Joshua 1:7, NIV). Thus, as they approach Ai, the second great city, they do not receive instruction from God. Nor, it seems from verses 3–4, do they treat the forthcoming battle at Ai as a serious challenge, much less as a divine campaign. Defeat and disaster ensue.

When Joshua consults God, however, a deeper reason for the defeat is revealed. One of the soldiers, Achan, has disobeyed the decree to destroy Jericho totally and has stolen some of the plunder. He admits that the reason for the theft is that he coveted the goods, breaking the tenth commandment (Exodus 20:17). Note that his sin is not simply personal; it corrupts the whole nation. Verse 1 states that 'the Israelites' were unfaithful, not just Achan himself. Achan fully understood his guilt: he hid the items in his tent (v. 21).

The reason for destroying the enemy's goods was not that they were evil. Rather, they are repeatedly described as being 'devoted' (vv. 1, 11–15), meaning set apart or reserved for God. The goods Achan coveted and stole belonged to God himself. Niditch, in *War in the Hebrew Bible*, sees this as a way to understand the whole concept of *herem*—as a form of sacrificial offering to God, dealing with the sin of Israel, not of the Canaanites.

The punishment on Achan and his family was severe. They were killed and the place where they died was named the Valley of Achor (Valley of Trouble) as a reminder of the spiritual danger that Israel had been in.

Taking further the idea that the story of the fall of Jericho is an echo of the creation story, Stern sees in the story of Achan's sin an echo of the serpent's actions in Genesis 3, bringing chaos into the created order and endangering the spiritual well-being of the whole creation.

The execution of Achan was not the end of the story, however. Centuries later, the prophet Hosea spoke of the Valley of Achor in terms of restoration and redemption: 'I will… make the Valley of Achor a door of hope' (2:15).

6 The danger of flattery

Joshua 9

After the destruction of Jericho and Ai, the strongest cities of the region, the Canaanites to the west realised that the Israelites were a military force to be reckoned with and could pick off the city states individually. The western states therefore came together in a coalition to confront the Israelites. However, the people of Gibeon tried a subtler approach. To avoid the fate of Jericho and Ai, and realising that the Israelites would not voluntarily make a treaty with a neighbouring nation, the Gibeonites disguised themselves as travellers from far away. Claiming that stories of the Israelites' victories had reached their distant land, they came begging a covenant treaty 'because of the name of the Lord your God' (v. 9). 'We are your servants,' they said (v. 8).

The Israelites' gullibility in falling for the scheme and agreeing to the treaty is attributed to the fact that, once again, they did not consult God before acting (v. 14). It is easy to see why they so readily succumbed to flattery. A generation before, they had been slaves in Egypt; a few weeks before, they had been wandering in the wilderness, and now they were enjoying an international reputation. However, the treaty was a serious divergence from God's plan, as they had been specifically forbidden to spare or make a covenant with any Canaanite tribe (Exodus 23:32–33).

Despite the subterfuge involved in the treaty, it was, like all ancient Near Eastern treaties, considered to be binding. However, once the trick was discovered, Joshua took steps to minimise its impact by making the Gibeonites slaves (their lands would later be allocated to the tribe of Benjamin) and giving them menial jobs to perform, preventing their assimilation wholly into Israel (v. 23).

This story helped to explain to later generations why, despite the *herem* decree by God, pockets of Canaanite population remained in Israel. There are also echoes of the story of the preservation of Rahab's family in Joshua 2. In both cases, the Israelites swear an oath of peace, and the Gibeonites' speech in verses 6–10 resembles the words of Rahab in Joshua 2:9–11. In particular, then, the story helped to explain the survival of the Gibeonites, their traditional trades of wood cutting and water carrying, and their later status as servants in the Jerusalem temple.

Guidelines

Already in our readings certain themes have emerged. In the battle against Ai and the dealings with the Gibeonites, we see the importance of listening to God and enquiring of him before we venture. We have seen the lesson on obedience hammered home. The Israelites have faced immense obstacles and tests—the waters of a great river, walled cities, flattery and their own sinful nature, and yet they have come through it all when they have listened to, obeyed and followed God.

It is worth reflecting this week on our own walk with God, and to what extent it involves obedience and listening for God's guidance. Although the Old Testament can sometimes seem simplistic in attributing success to obedience, and failure to disobedience, there is an important general principle at work. Christians are called to be obedient people. Romans 1:5 speaks of 'the obedience of faith' and Jesus himself said, 'You are my friends if you do what I command you' (John 15:14).

This rarely comes naturally or easily to us. Sometimes we appear to think that God is supposed to be obedient to our desires, rather than the other way round. But it is worth persevering. Norma Becker, the American Christian peace activist, wrote, 'The more we love God, the more we will obey. The more we obey, the more we will be aware of the reality of Christ in our lives. The more we are aware of Christ in our lives, the more victory we will experience. The more victory we experience, the less difficult the choices are and the less conflict we have within ourselves.'

Let us pray:

Lord, you call us to follow you, yet sometimes we do not follow as closely as we might. In our distance from you, we may not feel particularly courageous. At times like that, we need to hear your voice and the voices of others encouraging us. When we are tempted to succumb to flattery from around us or covetousness from within us, help us to be strong and loyal to the charge you have given us. Amen

1 The longest day

Joshua 10:1–15

Chapter 10 sees the campaign move to the south of the region. Jericho and Ai have been utterly destroyed, but the treaty with the Gibeonites has given Joshua a fortified base and skilled allies, changing the dynamic of the war, so the city states of the south join forces to attack the Gibeonites. Facing this large coalition, the Gibeonites immediately claim the protection guaranteed them by treaty. Joshua responds to the call, and the Israelites commit their whole army to the defence of Gibeon. Marching through the night, they catch the Amorite coalition by surprise and rout them.

Here in the narrative, two interventions by God take place, both of which emphasise God's power over the primordial forces and perhaps over the Canaanite gods, since the sun, moon and storms were all considered deities. First, a hailstorm rains down on the Amorites, killing more than are slaughtered in battle. Second, on Joshua's entreaty, the sun stands still, prolonging the time available for battle and enabling the victory to be completed. The prayer of Joshua in verses 12–13 was either taken from or recorded in 'the book of Jashar' (or the book of the just)— a lost book, quoted also in 2 Samuel 1:18, which seems to have been a collection of stories about Israelite heroes, at least partially in poetic form.

Most commentators focus on the astronomical issues involved in this event. Their suggested explanations have included an eclipse or a refraction or reflection of the setting sun's rays, whether a supernatural or natural phenomenon. Others have conjectured that the battle took place where there was a gap in the hills, which meant that sunset appeared to happen later. But the story is written to remind us, yet again, that this was not simply a human military conflict. God was fighting for Israel (v. 14).

Before we leave this story, it is worth pausing to consider the audacity and effectiveness of Joshua's prayer. For the narrator, the wonder of the event is not in the demonstration of God's power over nature but in the fact that God listened to such a prayer from a human being. In the very first reading in this series of notes, from Numbers 27, Joshua was told to enquire of God through Eleazar the priest rather than directly. In practice, however, even the narrator is in wonder at the effectiveness of Joshua's prayers.

2 War in the north

From the south of the region, the Israelites' attention moved to the north. This area had very different terrain and the challenges were different. The city states of the north did not have the huge fortress towns of the central plains, but their military forces were even stronger (v. 4) and they were politically more unified as a hegemony under the leadership of the king of Hazor.

Militarily, it is notable that each challenge faced by the Israelites was more demanding than the previous one. This campaign in the north was decisive and brutal. The principle of *herem* was applied to the people, to the military capability and to the dominant city of Hazor, which was utterly destroyed (v. 11). But the other cities—buildings, livestock and goods—were preserved. It is possible that these cities were left as a fulfilment of the prophecy in Deuteronomy 6:10 that Israel would be given 'fine, large cities that you did not build'.

With the defeat of the northern kings, the campaign was all but over. Some areas were still left unconquered (mainly the Philistine cities by the coast, 13:1–6), but the whole region was effectively under Israelite dominance. Chapter 12 lists 31 Canaanite kings who were killed in the campaign. This is an astonishing number in a region that measured some 50 by 15 miles, and it reflects how fragmented and divided the area was.

Verse 23 concludes the narrative of conquest and is a key summary of the whole book. Continuity with Moses is once again emphasised, reminding us that the command to conquer the land was originally conveyed through Moses (perhaps in Exodus 23:27–33). The second great task given to Joshua, to allocate the land, will move us on from this first section of the book, being covered in chapters 13—21. With the dominance of the Israelites, 'the land had rest from war' (v. 23), but it is worth remembering that a rest from war is not an end to war. Enmity between the Philistines, the remaining Canaanites and the Israelites endured, and, in many ways, this conflict shaped the region for generations to come.

3 Caleb's claim

Joshua 14:6–15

After the campaign was over, Joshua cast lots to allocate areas of the land to each of the Israelite tribes that settled there, as recorded in chapters 13—22. Those chapters are not without interest; they display the deep importance of land and roots to the people of Israel. In many respects, it is these narratives, not the stories of conquest, that represent the fulfilment of the promise given to Abraham in Genesis 12:7.

As well as territorial division, other allotments were made. Forty-eight cities were set aside for the priests and Levites (ch. 21), as Moses decreed in Numbers 35:1–8. Six of these levitical cities (three on the west and three on the east side of the River Jordan) were designated as cities of refuge, where a fugitive might find asylum (ch. 20). Joshua was given the city of Timnath-serah as a personal reward (19:49–50).

The remaining land was allocated to tribes by lot, but in Joshua 14, Caleb comes to Joshua to claim unspecified land that was promised to him as a reward for his faithfulness (Numbers 14:24). By birth, Caleb might not have expected much from the distribution of land. In 14:6 he is identified as descending from the Kenizzites, who were perhaps an Edomite people who had been assimilated into Israel. Caleb, however, rose to prominence in the tribe of Judah and was one of the spies sent by Moses into the land to scout it out. God decreed that, because of their faithful report, Joshua and Caleb would be the only members of their generation to live to settle in Canaan (Deuteronomy 1:36–38).

Caleb is now an old man and requests land for himself. Joshua gives him land around the large fortified city of Hebron, within the land allocated to Caleb's tribe of Judah. Hebron becomes one of the levitical cities of refuge (20:7).

This allocation of land was no sinecure. Ironically, many of the features of the land around Hebron were the very qualities that had led to the poor report by the other ten spies who scouted the land (Numbers 13:28). The hill country was inhospitable and, as chapter 13 recounts, not entirely subdued. Even at 85 years old, Caleb was not proposing an easy retirement.

A final feature of interest in this chapter is verse 10, which specifies the timeframe in which these events took place. Caleb was 40 when the promise was given to him (14:7). The Jordan was crossed 38 years later (Deuteronomy 2:14), and now a total of 45 years have passed. Thus, the conquest recorded in Joshua 1—11 took seven years.

4 Unity and loyalty

Joshua 23

After the allocation of the land, there was a period of peace that endured until Joshua was an old man and close to death. Like Moses before him (Deuteronomy 29—30), he summoned the people to hear his final words. This meeting may have taken place in Shiloh, where the ark of the covenant resided, or Shechem, the location mentioned in Joshua 24:1.

Joshua's speech begins with a reminder of Israel's recent history, which also serves as a summary of the book. The speech draws together some of the key theological themes that we have seen in our readings. There is a reminder that their success should be attributed to God, who has fought for them (v. 3) and kept all his promises (v. 14). There is a reminder to be obedient (v. 6) and that future success depends on this obedience (v. 16). But the people are called not just to obey dutifully, but to love God (v. 11). Several phrases in the speech echo the words spoken to Joshua at the beginning of the book. In verse 6 alone we see parallels such as the command to be strong (NIV), to obey the law of Moses, and not to turn to the right or the left (compare 1:6–7).

Often in the Old Testament, individual leaders, while important, are transitory, but the mission continues from generation to generation. The narrator has been at pains to show Joshua as the successor of Moses and the one to fulfil Moses' vision. In a sense, though, with the passing of Joshua this commission is democratised. Rather than being given to one individual, it is given to the 'elders and heads… judges and officers' of

Israel (v. 2). That paves the way for the continuation of the story in the book of Judges, which begins, 'After the death of Joshua, the Israelites inquired of the Lord, "Who shall go up first for us against the Canaanites, to fight against them?" The Lord said, "Judah shall go up. I hereby give the land into his hand"' (Judges 1:1–2). The responsibility no longer rests with one individual but with an entire people.

5 Covenant renewal

Joshua 24:1–28

Joshua chapters 1 and 23 serve as bookends, bracketing the story that is told in between. Joshua 24 is an appendix, recounting another speech given by Joshua and the renewal of the covenant at Shechem.

Shechem was an important centre for Israelite life and religion. Abraham confirmed the covenant and made a sacrifice there (Genesis 12), and the city would later serve as the first capital of the kingdom of Israel. Another renewal of the covenant had already been conducted there, as recorded in Joshua 8:30–35.

Joshua 24 is very formulaic, following the pattern of other ancient Near Eastern covenant texts, especially those found in Hittite treaties. Six features in the chapter reflect Hittite treaties.

- God is identified as the sponsor of the covenant (v. 2).
- Joshua reminds Israel what God has done for them, thus demanding their loyalty in return. Seventeen acts of God since the time of Abraham are recorded (vv. 2–13).
- Joshua outlines the duty that Israel owes to God—to fear him, serve him and be loyal to him (vv. 14–15).
- Provision is made for recording the covenant (vv. 25–26).
- There are to be witnesses to the agreement—the people themselves in the case of monotheistic Israel (v. 22), but gods in the case of Hittite treaties.
- Joshua lists blessings and curses that will come from keeping or violating the covenant.

Inserted into the covenant is a verse that has become one of the most famous in the Bible. Joshua lays the covenant terms before the people and commands them to choose whether to agree to it or not, but then says, 'As for me and my household, we will serve the Lord' (v. 15). This is something of a rhetorical device. Joshua is not giving them the option of sitting on the fence; they must commit themselves either to God or to their ancestral or Canaanite gods. Choice and loyalty are major themes throughout Joshua, where, as we have seen, loyalty to and trust in God are the only ways to guarantee success.

6 The death of Joshua

Joshua 24:29–33

With the end of the book of Joshua, a chapter in Israelite history comes to a close. Joshua died and was buried in his own city of Timnath-serah. The occasion is narrated with remarkably little detail or ceremony. Despite his long leadership of the whole people, at his death the only title recorded is that he was 'the servant of the Lord' (v. 29). In the book of Joshua this title has been repeatedly used of Moses, but this is the first and only time that it is given to Joshua himself. Some scholars have concluded that verses 29–33 must have been appended from a different source, which would explain the different description of Joshua. Whatever the source, however, this becomes one final way of marking the continuity between Moses and Joshua.

Moreover, perhaps Joshua's role in brokering the covenant between God and Israel, recorded earlier in the chapter, subtly altered his own status. He was not just a political and military leader; he was now a 'servant of the Lord', setting in order the relationship between God and Israel through covenant. His epitaph is seen in the consequences of his leadership: during his life and even through the next generation of leadership, the people remained true to the covenant (v. 31).

Another part of the biblical narrative reaches its closure in verse 32. Genesis 50:25 tells us that the Israelites promised Joseph that his bones would be taken out of Egypt; Exodus 13:19 records how Moses kept this vow and took them across the Red Sea. Now, the bones of Joseph are finally laid to rest in a plot of land long associated with the patriarchs.

The third funeral recorded is that of Eleazar the high priest, who is succeeded by his son Phineas. Eleazar and Joshua parallel Aaron and Moses, whose deaths are recorded in similar fashion in Deuteronomy 10:6 and 34:5–6.

With these three funerals, a generation of leadership passes away. More than that, the burial of Joseph's bones brings closure to the whole patriarchal period and prepares us for the opening of a new phase in Israel's history and relationship to God. Next comes the period of the Judges, during which the nation will move towards becoming a single kingdom with a centralised temple system, taking on, for good or ill, many of the features of the nations they have spent many years displacing.

Guidelines

Sometimes, when we want to make a judgement, we draw up a list of pros and cons, good qualities and bad, risks and opportunities. When we look back at Joshua's life, what is our final assessment?

There are elements in Joshua's character that are hard to warm to. He was uncompromising and could be merciless. He lived in a brutal time and, in some ways, reflected that age.

Equally, there is a lot about Joshua that is admirable. He was a natural leader, capable of inspiring and rousing people. He was an optimist, confident in his people and his God. He was capable of mistakes (he overreached himself in the battle at Ai, for example), but we do not see him making the same mistakes over and over again. He was capable of standing against popular opinion in order to do what he felt was right. Nowhere in Joshua's story do we see him arguing with God or refusing to do what was demanded of him. His faith and trust in God were rock solid. It was said at the end of Joshua's life that under his leadership 'not one of all the good promises that the Lord had made to the house of Israel had failed; all came to pass' (Joshua 21:45). It is worth pondering whether our lives or our leadership would receive such a positive assessment.

Ultimately, the lesson of Joshua is a lesson in faithfulness, demonstrated by his determination that even if nobody else goes with him, he will follow God: 'You choose… but as for me and my household, we will serve the Lord.' At times in the book of Joshua, as in our lives, God's hand is plainly visible, his guidance is clear and his intentions are obvious. Those times are all too rare. More often, God's plan is clear only in hindsight, if at all. These are the uncertain times when we need some of the trust in God that Joshua showed.

So let us pray:

Lord, thank you that we do not walk alone on the path you have set for us. Others walk alongside us, and, even if they fail us, you have promised never to leave us or forsake us. Help us to be faithful to you and to be true to our calling, whether it proves popular or whether we feel as if we are standing alone. And when people look back on our lives, may we be worthy to be called 'servants of the Lord'. Amen

---

FURTHER READING

Richard D, Nelson, *Joshua* (Old Testament Library), Westminster John Knox, 1997.

P. Stern, *The Biblical Herem: A window on Israel's religious experience*, Scholar's Press, 1991.

S. Niditch, *War in the Hebrew Bible: A study in the ethics of violence*, Oxford University Press, 1993.

Micah

The heading to the book of Micah tells us that this prophet (one of the so-called minor prophets, whose words together form the Book of the Twelve) was from Moresheth, a small town in the kingdom of Judah, not too far from the city of Jerusalem. We know nothing else about him—his age, how he earned his living, or how he came to believe that he was called to speak in the name of the Lord. The book's focus is overwhelmingly on its message rather than its messenger.

The oldest parts of the Micah tradition—mostly in the first three of the book's seven chapters—are associated with the eighth century BC, while the latter half of the book reflects the interests of exilic and post-exilic contributors and their efforts to explain the continuing relevance of this earlier tradition. There is little to help us ascertain a specific date or context for most of its contents. Other than the three kings named in 1:1, there are no specific references to people or events, just a general antipathy toward Jerusalem and its elites, supplemented by expressions of hope for a future of restoration. Indeed, Micah seems to be one of the Bible's more peripheral prophets—not in terms of the book's (in)significance, but in the sense that it speaks from outside the established social and political power structures (in contrast, for example, to the prophet Isaiah, who has ready access to kings and to the temple).

Biblical quotations are taken from the New Revised Standard Version.

1 Judgement against Samaria

Micah 1:2–7

As the book's heading observes, its message is concerned not only with the affairs of the city of Jerusalem, the capital of the southern kingdom of Judah, but also with the affairs of the city of Samaria, the capital of the northern kingdom (which the biblical texts often refer to as Israel). In the eighth century, the northern and southern kingdoms were two separate political entities—at odds over, among other things, the most judicious response to the growing might of the Assyrian empire.

As we get caught up in the great biblical narrative of the Old Testament, which tells how the Israelites were brought out of Egypt to be God's own people and lived in the promised land first under the judges and later under David and Solomon, it is easy to forget that it is not obvious why a prophet from Judah would be interested in Samaria and its inhabitants. If ever there was a political unity between these two kingdoms—a unity probably dominated by the north, with its powerful Omride dynasty, rather than the south, with its weaker Davidic dynasty—it was ancient history by the time of Micah.

In this passage, the connection seems to be rooted in a shared worship of the Lord, which (at least from the perspective of this southern prophet) the northern inhabitants of Samaria have betrayed through the worship of other gods or the improper worship of the Lord. This is one of the most common complaints of the prophets, whose concerns in this quarter suggest a perpetual issue in the habits of their audiences. Here, the consequence of Samaria's religious failings will be its political destruction. It is useful to recall that the political and the theological were coterminous in the ancient world. Therefore, the logical connection between a religious offence and a political or military punishment did not need to be spelt out.

Elsewhere, including in parts of Deuteronomy, this logic is premised on the idea that the Lord is the *only* god of the land (rather than simply the foremost of many gods worshipped in the region). The people who reside within its borders must worship the Lord and the Lord alone, or risk expulsion from it.

2 The doom of the cities of Judah

Micah 1:8–16

The transitional material in verses 8–9 suggests that the attention to the offences of the northern kingdom (1:5–7) may have been included in the book as a warning to the inhabitants of the southern kingdom. Their similar failings have become so widespread that they have reached

Judah's very heart—its capital city, Jerusalem, which is summoned here to witness their grim consequences.

The following verses reel through a dozen cities and towns—some large and well-known even today, others quite unknown to us—in a chaotic whirlwind tour around Judah. There is no apparent geographical logic to the sequence, despite numerous efforts among scholars to discern one. Although the passage neglects the details of the offences, aside from an enigmatic reference to 'the transgressions of Israel' in verse 13, it seems intent on emphasising the thoroughgoing nature of the cancer now afflicting Judah. The images thrown up by the opening verses, which are short and staccato, verging on incoherence, reflect the language and rituals of grief. Perhaps the failure to weep, in verse 10, reflects the insensibility that attends its most extreme instances.

We, Jerusalem, are treated to a tour of the devastation that our misdeeds have wrought, or will wreak. Tense is often fluid in prophetic texts, as the prophet's certainty about the future consequences of present behaviour manifests itself in the use of perfect tenses. The devastation includes humiliation, acute distress and overwhelming grief. If the details of the misdeeds are vague or convoluted (and attempts to trace the shifting identity of Israel in the latter half of the section only highlight our confusion), the ultimate consequences are anything but. Jerusalem's 'children'—all these towns and their inhabitants—have suffered as a result of Jerusalem's errors. Their suffering is not isolated from the fate of Jerusalem, but is intimately entwined with it. Jerusalem will grieve alongside them: the city's suffering is evoked by a reference to the shaving of the head, which, though ultimately forbidden by Deuteronomy 14:1, was previously a widespread mourning ritual.

3 Social evils denounced

Micah 2:1–11

Only in Micah 2 do we gain specific information about the offences by which Jerusalem and its inhabitants have invoked the divine fury. Perhaps surprisingly, the issue is not that the Jerusalemites have been worshipping other gods. This sort of theological disloyalty would be enough to drive even the most tolerant deity to the end of his tether, and it does indeed provoke significant divine displeasure elsewhere, because it implies a lack of trust in the Lord's provision and care. The problem is that they have been devising and carrying out various forms of injustice.

The accusations, though sweeping, are not generic. Rather, the abuses in question have arisen as a result of the particular circumstances and opportunities of the context. Free from significant military threats, the atmosphere of the eighth century was one of peace and physical security. This political calm rendered the region ripe for commercial development and fostered the growth of a small, wealthy upper class. Jerusalem, as a leading city of Judah, was the centre of the country's economic elite, over-laid with the political and religious powers of the capital. (Lachish was probably another major hub, which perhaps explains its particular place in 1:13.) Jerusalem's inhabitants not only represented the economically privileged; they constituted those with the means to ensure the continuation of their commercial advantages.

It is no coincidence, then, that the prophetic word here singles out the sin of greed. Although the command 'You must not steal' may be standard ethical fare, this offence is magnified by the lack of any extenuating circumstances: the accused purloin property not because they are in need but simply because they can (v. 1). What is more, this is theft at its most egregious: fields and houses (v. 2) constitute livelihoods, so their theft marks not mere physical loss but deprivation of families' means of survival.

The accused even target the most vulnerable members of society, its women and children (v. 9). At its most fundamental level, the crime of which the audience is accused is abuse of power. Although we see them directed at the weaknesses of an ancient audience, these concerns are just as provocative today, as the beneficiaries of our modern economic system face similar temptations to abuse positions of power for personal gain.

4 A promise for the remnant of Israel

Micah 2:12–13

In the midst of this condemnation comes a short interlude containing a promise. Commentators do not agree on whether the eighth-century prophet Micah would have included a hopeful element of this kind in his message to his contemporaries. Although most 19th- and 20th-century scholars considered the ('true') pre-exilic prophets to have been harbingers solely of doom, it has been more recently recognised that these prophets may have been encouraged to include an element of hope, so as to meet the objectives of prophetic proclamation. That is, while sometimes the purpose of the prophetic word seems to have been explanatory, justifying the current situation in terms of punishment for previous misdeeds, there is also the intention to be preventative. The word is designed to warn the prophets' audiences of the consequences of their current behaviour, in an attempt to persuade them to change it.

In this framework, holding out the offer of hope for those who respond to the prophetic word and reform would make sense. The prophet Micah, then, may have included some more positive elements in his message to the Jerusalemites as he endeavoured to persuade them to change their ways. Having said that, this attempt at persuasion was unlikely to have been the main focus of Micah's rhetorical efforts. The negativity of his message was apparently still remembered 100 years later, in Jeremiah's time: in Jeremiah 26:17–19 Micah is mentioned as a precedent for Jeremiah's own negativity, referring specifically to the judgement on Jerusalem in Micah 3:12.

The language of the promise in verses 12–13 draws on a pair of central metaphors for God: the image of the shepherd and the image of the king. In fact, these images are closely interrelated: ancient Near Eastern kings often depicted themselves as shepherds of their flock, guarding their people against invaders and ensuring that they were well fed and well cared for. The depiction of the Lord as Israel's shepherd and king here perhaps plays especially on the failures of Jerusalem's human rulers, which are detailed in the preceding and following passages. Although mortal kings and human princes may abandon or betray Israel in the present, in the future the Lord will care for Israel directly.

5 Wicked rulers and prophets

Micah 3

After this brief respite, Micah 3 resumes the earlier focus on the short-comings of the elite. Note that the audience is described as the 'heads of Jacob' (Jacob being a poetic name for Israel) and 'chiefs of the house of Israel' (vv. 1, 9). One of the challenges for understanding this text (and others like it) is that the biblical 'Israel' is an elusive and multivalent entity. Depending on context, it can refer to one or more of several different things. It may serve as an alternative name for the patriarch Jacob (in Genesis); as a collective name for the pre-settlement tribes (in Exodus to Judges); as the name of an ambitious political state ruled by David and Solomon (1 and 2 Samuel, and 1 Kings); as shorthand for the northern kingdom (1 and 2 Kings); or as the name of an idealised cultural or ethnic group, with variable political connotations depending on time and context. This usage is especially common in exilic and post-exilic texts, in the absence of an autonomous Judahite state.

In Micah, we have already seen 'Israel' mentioned in 1:13 as the source or model of transgression. Given the ire frequently directed at the transgressions of the northern kingdom, this might suggest that Micah was accusing people in Judah of having imitated the ill-doings of their northern neighbour (especially as this verse follows on the heels of the accusations against Samaria in 1:2–7). In 2:12, 'Israel' was used to refer to a future remnant community, under the direct authority of the Lord.

Here in chapter 3, the house of Israel seems to refer to the ruling elite in Jerusalem. It is there that the wrongdoings are located (vv. 9–10), and the confidence of the rulers, expressed in verse 11, reflects an expectation of inviolability which is especially associated with Jerusalem as the holy city of the Lord and the location of the Lord's temple. Here, the abuses of power have the particular tenor of arrogance: bribes and corruption are rampant, with no expectation of reprisals. Those who have the power to regulate the workings of justice—prophets (vv. 5, 11), priests and rulers (v. 11)—deliberately abuse it. Their rapacious greed strips those in their grasp of their livelihoods and dignity, degrading them, as if they were pieces of meat (v. 3). Human justice having been perverted, it is left to the Lord to execute divine justice (v. 12).

6 God's rule from Zion

Micah 4:1—5:1

From Micah 4 on, the book turns more robustly towards hope and promise. The image is of Jerusalem, also called Zion, as the centre of a new world order, ruled by the Lord in peace and prosperity. All peoples and nations, near and far, will attend to the authority that emanates from Jerusalem.

This picture is similar to the image of the restored Jerusalem painted by Isaiah 49—55, with all the world turned towards the Lord's capital city. Where there has been perceived weakness and slight, there will be strength and honour (4:6–7; compare the triumph of the blind and the deaf in Isaiah 42). Micah 4:1–3 is also nearly identical to Isaiah 2:2–4. Whether the similarity is because this depiction of the Lord's reign was a common one or because the editors of one of these books borrowed it from the other, in its present context it contributes to a picture of a future in which people will no longer fear for their survival or their livelihoods.

The imagery also echoes certain of the psalms, in which the just and righteous rule of the Davidic king is depicted as providing peace and security for peoples near and far. Here, again, the Lord has stepped into the void formed by human failings. Although the traditional structures of human authority have collapsed, the people may rely on the Lord; even in foreign exile, they will be protected from their enemies.

The rhetorical questions in verse 9 draw attention to the ultimate king. The image of the woman in labour draws on one of the most terrifying of everyday human experiences (one which, in precarious balance with its potential to bring forth life, could nevertheless bring death) to articulate the secure hold that the Lord has on Zion. Although the city and its inhabitants will face disaster, the Lord will bring them safely through.

Guidelines

The power of the prophetic literature lies in its ability to speak simultaneously in specifics and in universals. These chapters of Micah address particular historical circumstances, condemning specific (if unnamed and now unidentifiable) individuals and groups for specific betrayals of the

Lord's expectations. At the same time, it is the universal significance of these imprecations—their concern for society's most vulnerable and its leaders' just exercise of power—which has provided material for subsequent theological reflection and granted them an ongoing place in first Judahite, then Jewish and Christian tradition.

Nearly every prophetic book includes at least some indication of historical context—even if only a brief one, as with Micah—and thereby emphasises the significance of the historical origins and location of the prophetic words which these books preserve. At the same time, they reflect an openness to the ongoing significance of the prophetic voice for subsequent historical contexts. Injustice and abuses of power exist in many times and places; exile, displacement and fear of the unknown have inspired hopeful visions of a better future in every era. The recognition that the prophetic word may continue to speak again and again is most apparent in these books' final forms. Their textual, literary and theological complexity reflects successive generations' contributions of additional material, clarifying the prophetic word's continuing relevance for a new audience—much in the way that ministers today use sermons, blog posts and newsletters to explain the significance of biblical texts for our own generation.

27 March–2 April

1 The ruler from Bethlehem

Micah 5:2–6

Among Christians, this is perhaps one of the most well-known passages of the book of Micah, read each year as part of the Christmas liturgy. Its language echoes much of the preceding text, including the labour image from Micah 4, which here again is used to signal safe passage through travail (v. 3). Unlike the preceding promissory material, which focused on the kingship of the Lord in recompense for the failings of Israel's human leaders, this passage promises a human ruler. The first and most prominent aspect of this ruler's commission is to nourish and protect the people. If necessary, this protection may entail defence against invasion

(vv. 5–6). Note that, though obviously military in nature, the defence is described in a manner that evokes the shepherd's protection of his sheep.

As already noted, the image of the shepherd who cares for and protects his flock was an important way of describing an ideal king, emphasising his pastoral responsibility for the well-being of his people. In 2:12–13 we saw this royal image used to describe the Lord. Throughout the biblical text (most especially in the psalms, such as Psalms 18 and 89) there is a great deal of such dual imagery. It reflects not only the notion of the Lord as the ultimate, divine king (the ultimate sovereign, supremely right and just, the matchless protector of his people) but also the expectation that a truly just and righteous human king represents the Lord in his care for the people. The promise of such an exemplary ruler counters the disastrous failures recounted in Micah 3, and, given the focus of the earlier chapters on the shortcomings of the Jerusalemite elites, the emphasis in verse 2 on this king's humble origins is pointed.

The reference to Assyria (vv. 5–6) perhaps suggests the passage's origins in the eighth century, when invasion was a major concern; the hope for a king who would protect the Lord's people from danger is reflected also in the birth oracle of Isaiah 7:14–16. The fact that both of these passages are read at Christmas time highlights the perpetually precarious nature of human existence, always susceptible to those who seek greater earthly power. Unlike a human king whose reign will come to an end, the Christ will reign and protect the Lord's people in perpetuity.

2 The future role of the remnant

Micah 5:7–15

Verses 8–9 invert the shepherding imagery, depicting Israel not as the flock over which the just king will rule but as the lion that threatens the sheep. The reason for the difference is the location of the remnant. Whereas the preceding verses presumed that Israel was in its homeland, in danger from encroaching outsiders, these verses speak of an Israel dispersed among the nations. We can imagine the fearfulness of the audience: in a foreign land, surrounded by strangers—strange language, strange dress, strange customs, strange gods—they are a fragmented community which has been forcibly uprooted from its homeland and deposited in an unfamiliar environment.

Under foreign domination, Judah's former political, economic and religious elite were stripped of their power. The depiction of this remnant as a young lion works to reassure the audience that they will not be downtrodden for ever (while perhaps also playing on the royal associations of leonine imagery). Yet the violent, almost militaristic triumphalism of the image is cut off nearly as soon as it is broached, as the following verses recount a series of warnings about certain forms of divination and image-based worship.

This concern about religious matters is not otherwise particularly prominent in the book of Micah, which warns of and then explains the kingdom's downfall in terms of its leaders' moral shortcomings. It is much more typical of texts such as Deuteronomy and Kings, which explain the destruction of Judah as the Lord's punishment for the people's worship of other gods. The presence of such material in Micah perhaps reflects the role of authors and editors who had this mindset (often referred to as 'deuteronomistic' because of its links to the exclusive, centralised worship emphasised in the book of Deuteronomy) in the preservation and revision of many of the prophetic books. In the current context it reiterates the fault of the audience in having brought about their current state of exile, thus mitigating the temptation to belligerence.

3 God challenges Israel

Micah 6:1–5

These verses use a kind of prophetic speech known as the 'dispute', which appears to have been modelled on the form of argumentation used in legal cases. The Lord takes the role of prosecutor and judge, arrayed against the defendant. The created order (an order created by the Lord) acts as witness. The form is frequently used by Second Isaiah (for example, 41:21–29; 43:8–13), where the defendants are various other gods, whose silence in response to the Lord's summons is taken as evidence of their feebleness or non-existence. Here the defendant is Israel, whom the Lord summons to plead its case.

Although the crimes of which Israel is accused are not specified, the previous chapters of the book might lead us to imagine that they include the social and economic injustices that play such a significant role in the book's message, or Israel's failure to worship the Lord exclusively. The open-endedness of the summons leaves scope for the audience's own conscience: for what deeds might the Lord be demanding an account?

Twice Israel is called to explain itself; twice there is silence. There is no explanation, no justification, for its behaviour. The Lord's response to this silence emphasises the defendants' culpability. Far from having burdened the people with unrealistic expectations or unjustly inflicted suffering upon them, the Lord is the liberator, the God who cares about the sufferings of the people. He cares to such a degree that he has intervened in the affairs of powerful nations and kingdoms, bringing Israel out of the misery of Egyptian slavery and sending them leaders able to guide them in the right ways of living.

The effect of the dispute is manifold. Israel's inability to justify its actions emphasises its own responsibility for its current situation. At the same time, the people are reminded that theirs is a God who acts on their behalf, to save them from their enemies, and provides for them. Verse 5, with its invocation of the story about the foreign king Balak and his prophet Balaam (Numbers 22—24), reiterates that now, as then, the Lord will act; they must not despair.

4 What God requires

Micah 6:6–16

Micah 6:8 is one of the most well-known verses in the book, as it lays out in memorable phrasing the foundations of the good life, lived according to the instruction of the Lord. The word translated 'kindness' or 'loving kindness' is used elsewhere (for example, in the book of Ruth) to evoke the loyalty and devotion of familial bonds. Paired with the invocation of justice, the phrasing suggests that to 'do justice' means to treat all people with the attention and care that we most naturally reserve for our closest family members.

The emphasis on doing justice and on humility, the antithesis to the pursuit and abuse of power, is in keeping with the book's earlier condemnations. Those people who wield wealth and power use their advantage to cheat and lie—but, the passage promises, they will not be left unchecked for ever. All the wealth and all the power that they accumulate will ultimately be of no benefit to them. In the face of judgement, all their machinations will be useless.

The passage contrasts those who live out their commitment to the Lord in their ordinary daily lives with those who rely on superficial acts of piety to paper over their sins. Although many of the prophets (Amos and Isaiah, as well as Micah) railed against the activities of the religious system of their day, they did so not because they rejected the significance of acts of worship, and not because they rejected the need for religious institutions and officials. Their targets were those who performed the prescribed rites and rituals without reflecting the significance of those rites in their daily lived experience—the ancient equivalent of what might today be called 'Sunday Christians'. Sacrifices, libations, genuflections, rote recitation of the prescribed prayers—all of these are in vain if they fail to imbue a person's life with the ultimate reality that they reflect.

5 The prophet's lamentation

Micah 7:1–10

The lamentation in these verses expresses the disappointment of a prophet who sees all his efforts to sway the hearts and minds of his audience as a failure, and the grief of a man who knows the terrible fate that awaits his people. Similar distress is voiced in the lamentations or 'confessions' of the book of Jeremiah (chs 11—20), in which the frustrations of the prophetic speaker at his inability to effect meaningful change in his audience, and thereby to avert the threatened disaster, are so acute as to verge on uncontrolled rage at the Lord, who has not softened the people's hearts to make them more receptive to the prophetic message. In Jeremiah as well as Micah, the grief expressed by the prophet mirrors the grief of the Lord at the unresponsiveness of the people.

The speaker in many of these passages is ambiguous: the first person 'I' could be the prophet or could be the Lord. Here in this chapter, verse 7 eventually signals that this is the prophet's lament, but until that moment the text has been leaving its audience in limbo.

The crimes of which the people are guilty are again those involving the betrayal of justice, including bribery, abuse of power and lies. Even the bonds of familial devotion mean nothing: the father cannot trust his son, and the mother will be betrayed by her daughter. In this patrilocal society, the daughter-in-law would have moved out of her father's house and into her husband's family sphere upon her marriage. She represents the wider family loyalties that were achieved and cemented through intermarriage, which might have been relied upon to supplement the support and resources of the family in difficult times. All such security is lost, as it becomes a casualty of the same deceitfulness that has brought about the coming disaster. Social collapse will be complete and military destruction lurks in the background; injustice is both their cause and their consequence.

6 A historical appeal

Micah 7:11–20

Appropriately enough, the last section of Micah looks hopefully towards the future, albeit with one eye firmly on the past. Egypt and Assyria represent the ends of the known world, so the extension of dominion (ambiguously, either the people's or the Lord's) to include these lands represents its extension throughout creation.

As is frequent in the so-called historical psalms, the prophetic voice summons the Lord to act in favour of the people by appealing to the Lord's similar deeds in the past (vv. 14–15). As the Lord did for the people before, surely the Lord will do for the people again. First, the Lord is reminded of the mighty acts undertaken in bringing Israel out of the land of Egypt. Although an exilic context is not explicit here, it is present just under the surface. The role of God's people in relation to other nations was an immediate concern almost as soon as they were scattered among them. Establishing the reputation of the Lord in the eyes of these other nations was equally pressing: the destruction of Jerusalem and the dispersion of the Lord's people across the face of the earth were easily interpreted as an indication of the Lord's failure to protect the people against the might of the Babylonian empire and its gods.

The plea to the Lord to restore the people—a second exodus, akin to that envisioned by Isaiah 43—is not only for the sake of the people's welfare, although this is undoubtedly important (note again the image of the protecting and provisioning shepherd). The plea is also made so that the nations will see and acknowledge the true might of the Lord.

The final verses invoke the antiquity of the Lord's relationship with the people—generation upon generation, all the way back to Abraham—to remind the Lord that, for all the people's failures and shortcomings, forgiveness and compassion have been the overriding characteristics of this relationship. Although the people may fail again and again, with their loyalties tested and found wanting, the loyalty of the Lord is unsurpassed.

Guidelines

As low-profile as the book of Micah is—seven short chapters tucked in the middle of the smaller and easily overlooked prophetic books—most of us will recognise a good proportion of it, including the verse about what the Lord requires (6:8), the oracle about the birth of a new ruler (5:2), and the declaration that 'they shall beat their swords into plough-shares and their spears into pruning-hooks' (4:3). Although the various sections address it from different angles and with different emphases, the book's concern with justice strikes a consistent note throughout.

The persistence of this material in our consciousness reflects its powerful resonance with the lived experience of generation after generation—the longing for an era of peace and security, unmarred by the violent warring of states and tribes; the hope for kings, princes, presidents and prime ministers who seek the welfare of their people rather than their own advantage; and the acknowledgement that aspiration to power and the temptation to abuse it lurks just under the surface of most human lives.

It is tempting to read the book of Micah, with its vivid imagery and passionate entreaties, as expressing the righteous indignation of the weak against the strong. We may then naturally ally ourselves with the former and distance ourselves from the latter. Yet, in some part of each of our lives, we stand in a position of power—perhaps as government official or corporate executive, but also as parent, teacher, sibling, spouse or friend. The power of the book of Micah lies in its ability not only to function as a rallying cry in our efforts to condemn and rectify the injustices, dogmatism and pride of others, but as a reminder to reject and amend these traits within ourselves.

FURTHER READING

Ehud Ben Zvi, *Micah*, Eerdmans, 2000.

Jan Christian Gertz, Angelika Berlejung, Konrad Schmid and Markus Witte, *Handbook of the Old Testament: An introduction to the literature, religion and history of the Old Testament*, T&T Clark, 2012.

Daniel J. Simundson, *Hosea, Joel, Amos, Obadiah, Jonah, Micah*, Abingdon Press, 2005.

Ralph L. Smith, *Micah—Malachi*, Thomas Nelson, 1984.

Bruce K. Waltke, *A Commentary on Micah*, Eerdmans, 2007.

'We have seen his glory' (John 18—20)

Our chapters for the next fortnight are John 18—20, which contain the narrative of Jesus' arrest, trials, crucifixion, burial and resurrection, yet I have titled it 'We have seen his glory'. Why? The cross might be necessary to bring about good, but we don't easily think of it as a place of glory. However, there are hints that it should be seen as just that. The account of the two terrorists crucified 'one on his right and one on his left' (Mark 15:27) reminds us of James' and John's request: 'Let one of us sit at your right and the other at your left *in your glory*' (Mark 10:37). The first time in Mark that a human recognises Jesus as 'Son of God' is when the executioner 'saw how he died' (15:39).

John develops these threads, in keeping with his overall approach of making clear what might not have been understood at the time, but which the Holy Spirit later made clear (see, for example, John 14:26). Throughout the first eleven chapters of John, we hear that Jesus' 'hour' has not yet come, and then, just before the Last Supper, we are told that it has arrived: 'The hour has come for the Son of Man to be glorified... Now my heart is troubled, and what should I say? "Father, save me from this hour"? No, it was for this reason I came to this hour. Father, glorify your name!' (12:23, 27–28). The rejected prayer, 'Save me from this hour', makes clear that 'the hour' is indeed the crucifixion, not the resurrection. That is the moment of judgement when the 'prince of this world' is driven out (12:31).

The climax of John's prologue is, 'The Word became flesh and made his dwelling among us. We have seen his glory, the glory of the one and only Son, who came from the Father' (John 1:14). When was Jesus' glory as God's Son seen? Perhaps in part throughout the time when Jesus lived among them. Yet we should also connect the threads: Jesus' hour, when he displays God's glory, is the moment when he is lifted up on the cross (12:32). This is our God. So, over the next two weeks we will look right into the face of God, and we will see his glory in the account of Jesus' death.

Biblical quotations are taken from the New International Version.

1 Gethsemane

John 18:1–9

'Who is it you want?' asks Jesus; 'Jesus of Nazareth,' say the soldiers. Not once but twice, the soldiers make this declaration. It's deeply ironic, for of course they do not 'want' Jesus as a response of faith. This takes us back to John 12:20–21, where some Greeks arrive, wanting to 'see Jesus'. Their request leads into the verses about 'the hour' that I quoted above, in the introduction. The whole world 'wants' Jesus (as his opponents testify in 12:19), but hidden behind that 'wanting' is a response, a decision and, in effect, judgement (3:17–18).

Many commentators see in Jesus' words 'I am he' (v. 5, literally 'I am') an echo of the divine name revealed in Exodus 3:14. Although it's a perfectly normal Greek reply to the question, the way the soldiers retreat and fall to the ground (v. 6) certainly doesn't seem a normal response to a suspect who says, 'That's me.' It does sound like a response to a revelation of divine power or presence. It is almost as if all who want to see Jesus do indeed see something of his glory; sadly, though, recognition of Jesus does not always produce a response of faith: 'light has come into the world, but people loved darkness' (John 3:19).

We can take this point even further. The soldiers want Jesus, and he goes out to them and reveals himself to them. This is not to Jesus' benefit, but it is, potentially, to theirs. Jesus responds to those who seek him; he makes himself vulnerable to them, as he has done throughout his ministry. He is the one 'sent' into the world. This principle that Jesus reveals himself to those who seek him, regardless of their motives, should give us hope for our world.

Of course, we are also sent, just as Jesus was (John 20:21), and Jesus did indeed say that we are sent out 'like sheep among wolves' (Matthew 10:16). Are we called to respond to those who seek, to make ourselves vulnerable, even if it may not be to our benefit?

2 One man dying

John 18:10–14

'The cup' (v. 11) is not mentioned elsewhere in John's Gospel. However, it features in the passage about James and John and the places on Jesus' left and right in his glory (Mark 10:38–39), and it is the focus of Jesus' mental battle in Gethsemane (Mark 14:36). Jesus chooses to accept God's will, and his acceptance is put into stark contrast with Peter's resistance.

It is often hard to accept things that you have not shaped yourself; it is hard to be 'done to'. Often, that reluctance lies at the heart of conflict. The pastor, manager or parent who wants to bring about change gets frustrated by other people's resistance, not realising that the resistance is caused not really by disagreement over the plan, but by annoyance at being 'done to'. It's also why so many people in hospital just want to get home. We might imagine that they would feel more secure in hospital, with people looking after them, but they want to escape from being the recipient of others' actions, and get back to their own home where they can decide for themselves. Jesus, though, is willing to accept his Father's will. It is an expression of trust in God as well as of his own humility.

Caiaphas is right, of course: it is good for Jesus to die on behalf of the people (v. 14; see also 11:48–52). Once again we see John's irony: the soldiers 'wanted' Jesus, but not in the way they thought. Caiaphas is right that Jesus' death will benefit the people, but not in the way he imagines.

This points us to an intriguing phenomenon: God does seem to use people for purposes beyond their intention or recognition. I think I often see it happen. Someone provokes a crisis out of bad motives, and yet that crisis produces good outcomes; or wickedness arrogantly overreaches itself and causes the disengaged to wake up and fight it. I have noted over the years that God has used for my good what others have said to me, even when they were wrong! 'In all things God works for the good of those who love him' (Romans 8:28).

The ruthless expediency of Caiaphas and the oppressive use of power by the soldiers and authorities are turned upside down by Jesus' humility and willingness. Paradoxically, they lose all control when he chooses not to resist.

3 Speaking the truth

John 18:15–27

'I said nothing in secret' (v. 20). This is a powerful claim. Many of us spend much of our lives in a complex game of 'impression management', judging carefully what we reveal or hide from each different person or context. Of course, there are things appropriate to share with a close friend that would be inappropriate to discuss at work. However, many of us have a tendency to spin webs, trying to control what people know or think about us. 'Knowledge is power', so we like to control knowledge because we think it makes us powerful. We may also be ashamed of aspects of our lives, so we find ourselves forced into concealment and deception.

This passage provides two foils that show Jesus' truthfulness in greater clarity. Peter's denials are a fixed part of the Gospel story, but here in John we see no remorse or breakdown: this is not Peter's story but Jesus'. His lies and betrayal serve only to accentuate Jesus' truthfulness. Interestingly, many people have sympathy for Peter: we can all imagine the pressure he felt, the confusion, the fear. Indeed, people have explained to me that he did the right thing because it would have been pointless for him to have got himself arrested. Better to lie, stay free and so be able to help. Indeed, Peter is not wicked—he is normal, like us—but Jesus is different.

The second foil is the officer who strikes Jesus (vv. 22–23). This highlights how unwelcome truth-telling can be, because it shows up the rest of the situation for what it is. One person who refuses to take bribes, fiddle the expenses or massage their figures upsets the system in which those actions are routine.

It is also common for people to seek for 'secret truth'. The internet is full of conspiracy stories whose basic premise is 'They don't want you to know…'. People also welcome 'secret teaching' within their faith, longing for a preacher to tell them, 'The Greek really says…' or 'This suddenly becomes clear when you realise that people in those days did x'. But Jesus said nothing in secret. There are no secrets about him, and, if we are his disciples, we must surely strive to be just as transparent and honest.

4 What is truth?

John 18:28–38

Hypocrisy is deeply corrosive. If those who stand publicly for certain values privately contradict them, the values themselves are damaged. Even worse, the very idea of values becomes undermined and cynicism takes hold. People start to believe that any appeal to values is just a method for controlling others.

Our passage begins with a classic bit of hypocrisy: the Jewish leaders maintain the appearance of piety by not entering the Gentile palace, yet they are perfectly happy to do their self-serving deals with the Gentile authorities. In Jesus' words, it's like whitewashing a tomb (Matthew 23:27). This is a particular danger in any rule-based system. It is possible to keep the rules precisely, and hence be untroubled by conscience, while clearly going against their intention. So here, the leaders keep their rule about not associating with Gentile authorities while actually taking forward a plan in which those authorities are key allies.

Pilate resists being drawn into the game being played, although, as the chapter goes on, we see that his commitment to justice is only skin-deep. Presumably he knows he is being used as a pawn in the leaders' plan. At least, he can't be seen to be simply acting on their request; he has to maintain the appearance of being in charge.

This passage raises the questions: 'Who are Jesus' people?' and 'Where does he belong?' Pilate assumes that race and culture are what matter. Jesus is a Jew, so he should be judged by the Jewish leaders, and any claim to be 'King of the Jews' needs to be recognised by those leaders. This fits with the general Roman policy of allowing considerable self-governance for conquered peoples, as long as they paid their taxes and kept the peace. But Jesus refuses to accept this position. His status as 'king' is not dependent on human recognition (John 2:23–25), and his 'people' are not defined by their race but by their response to him (1:10–13).

Pilate's famous question 'What is truth?' cuts to the heart of the issue. Is truth absolute, standing above our human plans with their twists and turns, or is it a commodity to be used for our purposes? Rule-based ways of being pious turn to hypocrisy; expediency reduces truth to a tool for our use. Jesus stands for something different, which disturbed and frightened those around him, and still does.

5 We have a law

John 18:38—19:7

What a travesty of justice! Three times Jesus is declared innocent by the Roman governor, yet still he is tormented and is going to end up dead. 'We have a law,' claim the religious leaders, but there is no such law. The title 'God's son' could simply be a way of describing a pious Jew (Matthew 5:9) or a chosen king (2 Samuel 7:14; Psalm 2:7); it need imply nothing 'blasphemous'. Their appeal to the law is not about justice but about getting their own way.

Two themes dominate this horrible scene. First, there is the desire not to take responsibility. Pilate doesn't want to execute Jesus, but nor will he take responsibility for setting him free. The leaders want him dead, but are happy for someone else to do it. If we take literally Pilate's words 'You take him and crucify him' (v. 6), we see Pilate being prepared to bend the Roman principle that conquered people couldn't impose the death penalty, as a way of passing responsibility to the Jewish leaders. But they, of course, don't want that: at this moment, their position as conquered people is convenient.

Second, there is the fact that Jesus is being used. He is a pawn in a game between Pilate and the leaders. By presenting the bloodied Jesus wearing a thorn crown, with the mock acclamation, 'Here's the man!' Pilate is mocking the Jewish leaders and nation. This, he implies, is the only sort of king they are going to have, and all their hopes of nationhood are a joke. Meanwhile, the Jewish leaders enjoy forcing Pilate to release Barabbas, who is a revolutionary against Rome. In one sense, Jesus fades from the scene. It is his fate that is being decided, but centre stage is a game between Pilate and the Jewish leaders.

Sadly, neither of these two phenomena is far from our own lives. Passing the buck and dodging responsibility are common responses within our churches, families and workplaces, and in the political world. Often we get drawn into games where far more energy is spent on avoiding responsibility than on solving the problems. Also, Jesus continues to be used as a pawn. People claim that their agenda is 'Christian' and soon a fight ensues in which Jesus seems completely absent; just as in this passage, he is both ignored and harmed.

6 No king but Caesar

John 19:8–16

What does Jesus mean by the phrase 'guilty of a greater sin'? Presumably the point is that Pilate is guilty for failing to have courage as a human being and commitment to justice as a judge. He hands over for crucifixion someone who he believes should not be crucified. But the 'greater sin' lies with the religious authorities because they are the instigators of the whole business. Pilate is unjust and cowardly, yet he is legitimately the judge, with authority 'given from above' (v. 11; see Romans 13:1). It is the religious leaders who have usurped authority to speak for God. They have rejected what they should be accepting (John 1:11) and have decided for their own reasons that Jesus should die (John 11:47–53).

'We have no king but Caesar' (v. 15) puts the seal on the priests' betrayal. God is, or should be, their king. It's one thing perhaps to accept and adjust to Roman rule, but to proclaim that there is *no* king but Caesar is to reject God and Israel's calling. Even worse, here it is said in an effort to threaten Pilate, implying that they are the true and loyal Romans, not him (if he doesn't do as they want). In Mark 14:61–62, when Jesus quotes Daniel 7:13 to the high priest, he is effectively saying that the religious leaders are part not of 'God's people' but of the godless, oppressive empires depicted in the book of Daniel as beasts. In the proclamation, 'We have no king but Caesar,' they show that he was right.

None of this has anything to do with Jewish people today. The actions criticised are those of a particular group of people at a particular point in history. Indeed, there are many examples throughout history of Christian leaders manipulating civic authorities to implement their self-serving schemes, and of Christian churches sacrificing their loyalty to God on the altar of political gain.

Of course, we never do anything similar, do we? We never feel self-justified because, although we 'set something up' (whispering and engineering behind closed doors), it was actually someone else who did the deed. We never say things we don't mean because it will give us what we want; we don't play down our devotion to God in public, thinking that we can 'make it up' to him afterwards. Our consciences will tell us that, actually, we do.

Guidelines

Adam and Eve wanted to be like God, and so do we all. Perhaps we don't show this desire in dramatic ways, but we have a deep longing to control what happens around us. That longing is unsurprising—it seems to be intrinsic to human life—but what matters is where it takes us. This week we have seen a contrast. Jesus is true, transparent and humble, responding to everyone, whatever their intentions towards him. Humans are locked into games, hypocrisy and manipulation—judging situations, engineering them, responding differently to different people. He is light, but we live in the shadows because we think that those shadows give us room to present a 'better' version of ourselves.

Who are we fooling? Mainly ourselves. It isn't worth the effort, but it's hard to stop, because we fear that if we move from shadows to light, we may be judged, or be put at the mercy of other people's games—just as Jesus was.

'I have done nothing in secret,' said Jesus. Let us pray that God's Spirit would so change us that we might say the same. Perhaps there is one area of life in which you are being called to come into the light, to stop trying to control what others think of you.

1 Crucifixion

John 19:17–24

Barbaric and humiliating, crucifixion was intended not just to torture and kill, but to present a public spectacle of powerlessness. The Romans used it only against revolutionaries who tried to overturn the very order of society—slaves rebelling against their masters, and conquered people rebelling against the Romans.

Can this place of powerlessness be turned into the throne of glory? As we have seen, many threads in John's Gospel, building perhaps on the reference to places on Jesus' left and right in his glory (Mark 10:37), have pointed to this moment of 'lifting up' as 'the hour' when God's glory is manifest and the prince of this world is driven out. Could the spectacle of crucifixion, designed to assert the futility of challenging the powerful, be the moment when their power collapses? (See Colossians 2:15.)

Nothing in this passage confirms or points to that hope. The machinery of Roman terror just rolls on unchecked—except for one thing. There is a reference to the fulfilment of scripture in the way the clothes are divided (Psalm 22:18, from the psalm that begins, 'My God, my God, why have you forsaken me?'). If scripture is being fulfilled, then all is not out of control. God's purposes are being worked through.

This speaks to the reality of life. When all seems dark, there is no great shining beacon proclaiming, 'God is in control'. If there was, it wouldn't seem so dark. Powerlessness and despair are soul-destroying because, like crucifixion, they seem to laugh in scorn at human hopes and dreams. How can God be in control when such evil is happening? Yet, in a small whisper, we hear that God's purposes are being worked through; that what is happening is not outside God's sight; that this is not the end but is part of a bigger story.

Who knows what Pilate meant by the title he pinned to the cross? Perhaps he was mocking the Jewish authorities, proclaiming, 'This is the only sort of king the Jews will ever have'. Perhaps he was, in a strange way, honouring Jesus, having seen something in him that was more worthy of respect than anything his accusers had displayed. It doesn't matter. It is futile to find purpose or hope in the comments of those caught up in tragedy or human wickedness. We find them by noticing the connections between what is happening and God's bigger story.

2 Death

John 19:25–30

Love remains. In the horror of the cross, faith and hope seem to have failed. Yet, at this final moment before Jesus' death, we see love enduring: the three Marys stand close. It is sometimes said that it was safer for the women to be there than it would have been for the male disciples, although women face their own dangers from soldiers and among angry crowds and naked power. We should not undervalue their presence— their love overcoming their fear.

The theme of love is further enhanced by the reference to 'the disciple whom Jesus loved' (v. 26). This enigmatic figure appeared at the last supper (13:23) and will feature again at the empty tomb (20:2). Speculation abounds as to his identity. Perhaps he is even a representation of 'the ideal disciple', although that might make more sense if he were described as 'the disciple who loved Jesus'. The last verse of this Gospel seems to claim that this figure was its source (21:20–24). If the Gospel was written up after he had died (which 21:23 perhaps implies), this would be an intriguing but honouring way for his friends and followers to refer to him in the Gospel carrying his testimony.

Leaving such questions aside, though, we see love for Jesus transformed into new human relationships. People whose only link is a common love for Jesus become linked with each other using the language of the closest human bonds—child and mother. The centurion saw Jesus' glory as he died, recognising him as God's Son (Mark 15:39); here we see another aspect of God's glory—the creation of love and new hope in the place of brokenness.

'It is finished' (v. 30). It is done. It's over. Jesus' words can first be seen as the final words of a man who is thankful that his ordeal is over. In Gethsemane he chose to drink the cup that his Father had set for him (John 18:11). He has drunk the dregs and it is over. However, just as, without minimising the horror of the cross, we can recognise it as the place of glory and victory, so too the words 'It is done' or 'It is accomplished' speak of something great being achieved, despite or even through all this pain. Now that the ruler of this world has been driven out (12:31), eternal life is available (3:14–15) and will include many people (12:24).

3 Burial

John 19:31–42

We will touch on just three of the many elements in this reading. First, the 'water' that flowed from Jesus' side (vv. 33–35) is likely to have been the fluid that gathers in the lungs as suffocation takes place, or the fluid that gathers around the heart due to intense stress. Together with the soldiers' horrific professionalism, this points to the certainty that Jesus was dead. The explicit reference to the eyewitness (v. 35) confirms the importance of the fact that he genuinely died.

Second, Jesus' death provoked courage, love and dedication from Joseph and Nicodemus. They had every reason to be frightened: caring for the executed criminal, potentially creating a shrine for him, and giving his body a burial 'fit for a king' was far more dangerous than simply watching from the crowd, as the Twelve did. Terrible events often do produce love and courage, and, although these qualities in no way 'balance out' the wickedness of what happened, it is right to note them as signs of hope, like seeds sprouting in an old quarry or slag heap.

Third, the words 'They will look on the one they have pierced' (v. 37) fulfil the prophecy of Zechariah. It is revealing to read Zechariah 12:10 and 13:1: 'And I will pour out on the house of David and the inhabitants of Jerusalem a spirit of grace and supplication. They will look on me, the one they have pierced, and they will mourn… On that day a fountain will be opened to the house of David and the inhabitants of Jerusalem, to cleanse them from sin and impurity.' At this point when Jesus has been murdered through the manipulation of the religious leadership, the gospel speaks of grace and forgiveness.

The image of a 'fountain of forgiveness' springing up in the place of execution is a beautiful picture of God's triumph in the face of the assertion of power by the wicked. We should be careful not to think of the cross as the place where God's power proved greater than that of his enemies. The enemies won the 'power game', but God did something different, more important, through sacrifice and love. Indeed, there is irony in the fact that it was a Roman executioner, stabbing a victim to ensure he was dead, that released this flood.

4 Running

Mary assumed the worst. Not only had they tortured and murdered the one she admired and loved, but now they had broken into his tomb and stolen his corpse. It's understandable, given all she had been through, but a mistake to underestimate the potential for hope.

The account of what happened that morning builds up across the Gospels. In Mark we read of women finding the tomb open and hearing an angel speak to them. They then run away. In Matthew the story is the same, except that they run to tell the disciples. In Luke we hear the next piece: the male disciples don't believe the women's message, but Peter, at least, runs to the tomb, sees the 'linen strips' and goes away wondering. John 20 focuses on what happens when Peter arrives at the tomb. We gather that the disciple who was at the cross (19:26–27) is with him. The details are intriguing: the other disciple arrives first, but Peter goes in first; then the other one enters and 'believes'. Attempts to give meaning to this detail are unconvincing; perhaps we have to say that it just happened that way.

Verse 9 is strangely similar to the story of the disciples on the Emmaus road (Luke 24:13–33), where we learn that they too were unaware that scripture foretold the resurrection, but were forced to start considering it because of what they saw and heard. It's helpful to recognise that the resurrection was so unexpected and unlikely that people didn't believe in it easily. It was a unique event in the history of the universe—God breaking the power of death and reconciling the rebellious world to himself. Indeed, the personal miracle of coming to realise that God loves us with an unquenchable love is something that most of us find hard to take in.

In different ways we see Jesus' followers going through a sequence: hear, respond, believe, understand. Is that a pattern for most people as they they encounter God? Belief comes late in the sequence, and understanding right at the end. Our faith is not an intellectual exercise, in which understanding comes first and flows out into action. So often, as here at the resurrection, a response from our hearts to what we have seen, heard or perceived in the world around us comes first, and the intellect struggles to follow.

5 Reunion

Is this the most moving scene in the Bible? Quite possibly. Mary's grief is palpable: the friend and leader whom she deeply loves, who has transformed her life (Luke 8:2), has been tortured and murdered, and now she thinks his grave has been desecrated. No wonder she mistakes Jesus for the gardener. The finality of death means that the person she most wants to meet is the one she least expects.

There is nothing to be said. This is not a moment for words or explanations: reunion is all that matters. Mary has got back what she lost (as another Mary did, when she lost her son for three days at the temple at Passover many years before: Luke 2:41–50). All the way through Jesus' ministry, the personal relationship has been paramount. His call to the fishermen was 'Follow me', not 'Accept my teaching'; people's lives were transformed by *meeting* him. The same is true if we look more broadly at the Bible: for example, Job's questioning is satisfied not by answers but by meeting with God (Job 42:4–6).

This, though, is not the end of the story. Mary cannot cling on to Jesus, hug him, hold him and never let him go (v. 17), for there is still work to be done. She needs to be the messenger of Jesus' resurrection (v. 18)—or, as she was sometimes later to be called, the 'apostle to the apostles'. He needs to ascend to the Father, so that the Holy Spirit can be given (16:7) and even greater things can happen (14:12). Again, this is a pattern elsewhere in the Bible: revelation of God is, at the same time, a commission for action (see, for example, 1 Kings 19:12–17 and Isaiah in Isaiah 6:6–10). Similarly, after James, John and Peter had heard God's voice and seen Jesus transfigured, they had to go down the mountain and engage in the hard realities of life (Mark 9:2–29).

Even this is not the end of the story. Our hope is for a future reunion with Jesus when he returns (1 Thessalonians 4:17), and then, finally, he will be with us for ever. In the meantime, through prayer, worship, creation and the lives of others, we seek to see Jesus—even if only fleetingly—to sustain our hope and give joy to our hearts.

6 Seeing God's glory

John 20:19–31

The reunion continues. Jesus meets with the disciples, and later with Thomas, and they are transformed. Before these meetings, they were still frightened; afterwards they are filled with joy and are given new commissions—sent out to continue Jesus' work. They are given the Holy Spirit (the 'replacement Jesus', to ensure that they are not 'orphans': John 14:16–18), and, in particular, they are to be in the business of forgiveness.

There is no real criticism of Thomas's desire to see Jesus. After all, he was only asking for what the other disciples had received, and, indeed, Jesus responds to his request. We might argue about whether it was reasonable, whether Thomas ought to have believed anyway, or whether it was asking too much; but Jesus, it seems, is kinder than us and deals gently with Thomas's (and perhaps our) fears and hesitations. We might compare Jesus' encounter with the Syro-Phoenician woman, whose challenge to him was also treated kindly (Mark 7:24–30). God is not offended by our questions, requests and worries.

Jesus does, though, issue a challenge for us—that we should progress beyond Thomas's level (v. 29). Jesus may have sympathy with his weaknesses (Hebrews 4:15–16), yet we should aim for greater faith, to get to a point where our faith can sustain us even when the tangible proof of God's presence is absent. That call to 'progress' comes elsewhere in the New Testament too—for example, Hebrews 5:12—6:1 and 1 Corinthians 3:1–3.

Thomas's request to see and touch Jesus' wounds, and, indeed, Jesus' instruction to him to put his hand in the stab wound, can seem macabre and distasteful. However, maybe we should learn from it, noting that this request leads to the highest acclamation of Jesus in the Gospel: 'My Lord and my God' (v. 28). The wounds are not just a method of identification. They display Jesus' divinity, just as in Mark 15:39, his divinity is revealed as he dies.

God's essence is not power (however much philosophers might try to define God as 'omnipotent'); it is love and sacrifice. In the book of Revelation, in all likelihood by the same author, John hears (expects) that

God is a triumphant lion, but sees that the reality of God is a slaughtered lamb (Revelation 5:5–6). Even in heaven the wounds remain, because the cross is glory, not shame. In coming face to face with the wounds, Thomas sees Jesus' glory.

Guidelines

It is hard to write about Jesus' death and resurrection without sounding trite, or seeming to imply that suffering isn't really that bad, or that God wins in the end so all is OK—but that is to trivialise his death and resurrection, as well as human suffering. The truth is deeper and more disturbing. Seeds of love and hope appear in the midst of the pain; the stab of the spear releases a flood of forgiveness; the tomb is a place of reunion; the wounds are the true glory. If you want to see God, look at the man dying on the cross.

What does this mean? I don't know. It's too difficult for me to understand, but, as we have seen, understanding is overrated. We are called to respond. We must respond to the truths that God bore suffering and turned it to love and mercy, and that powerlessness was glory, not shame. Perhaps, in some small way, we can copy this pattern. Maybe we can even believe that this is indeed the deep way in which God's world works. Imagine what the world would be like if suffering and injustice produced love and forgiveness, not bitterness and hatred, and if power was seen as trivial—the stuff of childish games—compared with love and sacrifice. One day, when we meet Jesus, we might even understand it (1 Corinthians 13:8–12).

'We have seen his glory.' John's response was to share eternal life with others and to welcome them in love (1 John 1:2–3). What's yours?

Mission, cross and resurrection

In the previous issue of *Guidelines* we looked at 'Mission and incarnation', and in the next two weeks we look at the cross and resurrection in the same light.

The crucifixion of Jesus is the unique atoning event at the heart of God's salvation story. It is unrepeatable, an objective reference point in the history of humankind. Jesus' enigmatic cry 'It is finished' (John 19:30) captures that sense of absolute finality. Subjectively, though, the cross-event also provides us with a template for discipleship. We cannot, and need not, replicate Christ's sacrifice, but we must take seriously what it means to 'take up the cross daily' and follow him (Luke 9:23).

Over the centuries, Christians have wrestled with their understanding of the cross. Different theories of the atonement have been offered, each metaphor finding an echo in scripture and in the life of Christ. In the first week's readings I shall consider five ways in which the atonement has been understood historically. These notes will encourage us to engage with and evaluate each of these understandings of the cross from the perspective of our mission. I won't necessarily be saying which is right or wrong, but rather what each might help us to see as we consider mission in the light of the cross.

In the second week, we turn to the resurrection. Again, our understanding of this pivotal event must include objective and subjective elements. The resurrection is presented to us in the Gospels as a real physical phenomenon. Like the crucifixion, it stands as a turning point in the history of the world, overthrowing the whole cosmic order of things. It also transformed the first disciples' experience of faith, changing they way they thought, felt and acted—and it continues to do so for us, the followers of Jesus today. The mission of the church goes on in the power of the resurrection.

We begin our studies of the crucifixion, then, with a humble and contrite spirit. Humble, because all our theories of the atonement are ultimately inadequate, and there will probably be some models that you don't wholly agree with; but contrite too, because the cross of Christ and the sin of the reader are inextricably linked. The cross of which we speak, we ourselves have shaped.

Biblical quotations are from the New Revised Standard Version unless otherwise stated.

1 The atonement as example

1 Peter 2:11–25

We begin our studies (perhaps strangely, but for reasons we will see) with the atonement as example. Initially formulated by Socinus in the 16th century, this approach rejected older ideas of vicarious satisfaction. Rather, the emphasis was primarily on the death of Christ as the perfect example of how to live. Socinus cited 1 Peter 2:21: 'For to this you have been called, because Christ also suffered for you, leaving you an example, so that you should follow in his steps'. (See also 1 John 2:6: 'Whoever says, "I abide in him", ought to walk just as he walked.')

Behind this perspective, however, is a defective theology: Socinus did not believe that Jesus was divine. If Jesus is not ontologically different from us but just a better person, then being the perfect example is the highest virtue that can be attributed to him. It may seem strange that I have included this faulty perspective here, but I do so because it finds a resonance in today's world, where people are often willing to acknowledge Jesus as a great example but stop short of acknowledging his divinity.

While it is true that Christ does offer a unique and challenging example of how to live, this position ignores swathes of scripture. Indeed, just three verses after Socinus' favourite words comes verse 24: 'He himself bore our sins in his body on the cross, so that, free from sins, we might live for righteousness; by his wounds you have been healed.'

Here is the rub. When we engage in mission, whether among neighbours, friends, family members or people in faraway places, our longing is to be accepted, not rejected. There can be a temptation, therefore, to play down aspects of our faith that might offend people, even though we are told that the gospel *will* offend and will be a stumbling block to many.

If I find myself in a deep pit, along with a friend, it will inspire me if I see them scrambling their way out—but if I can't do what they have done, it is of no help to me. I need someone to get me out of the pit. Christ is without sin but we are not. We need someone to rescue us, not just inspire us, and that is true for today's generation too.

2 The atonement demonstrates God's love

2 Corinthians 5:1–21

The cross is an act of love or it is nothing. Love is often costly, and infinite love is infinitely costly. Developed by the French theologian Pierre Abélard (1079–1142), this approach emphasises the cross as a demonstration of God's love towards humankind, rather than as an act directed *at* God, satisfying any requirement for a sacrificial payment. The efficacy of the cross is seen in the way our fear of God and ignorance about God are removed when we see the extent of God's love for us in Christ. This, it is argued, aligns with the great scriptural affirmation that 'God is love' (1 John 4:8, and resonates with verses such as Luke 19:10 and 2 Corinthians 5:19: 'In Christ God was reconciling the world to himself, not counting their trespasses against them.'

There is great truth here. Consider for a moment the power of love in human relationships. A child's life is shaped hugely by the love of its parents, or, tragically, the lack of such love. The bond between lovers who meet and commit to each other is utterly transformative. We see God's great love on the cross, and so, it is argued, we can be transformed. Through this understanding of the cross, we are brought to a deep conviction about sin and repentance and a new openness to God. While Adam and Eve hid from God, and even though their sin bore consequences, it was God's approach to them that exemplified a love that will not let us go (Genesis 3:9). The prodigal son found the love of his father to the fore, not the requirement that his sin be atoned for (Luke 15:20). In Christ we see God approaching us sinful people—and, according to Abélard, his death is a consequence of his loving incarnation, not its primary purpose.

Perhaps what we are learning here is that mission is compromised without love. A pastor who does not love the people in their church will struggle. A mission worker who does not find space to love the people to whom they are sent will fail. Every Christian is called to love their neighbour—not primarily to preach to them, convert them, or invite them to church. The first and foremost call is to love them. That is the way of the cross.

3 The atonement demonstrates God's justice

Isaiah 42

This image was developed by the lawyer Hugo Grotius (1583–1645), and it represents a shift towards a God-centred view of the cross, in contrast with the previous two human-centred views. Sin transgresses God's universal holy laws, and God responds in ways that recognise both his love and his justice. He forgives, but does so in a way that upholds the severity of sin and maintains the moral order of the universe.

Grotius argues that Christ's death was not a penalty for sin but a substitute for the penalty of sin. He contends that a punishment cannot be transferred to an innocent person, as the connection between sin and guilt will then be severed. The cross was not, therefore, Christ's vicarious bearing of our exact, deserved punishment, but a demonstration of God's hatred for sin. So the cross both upholds the morality of the universe and allows God to forgive those who, moved by the gravity of sin, repent and ask for forgiveness.

The weakness of this view is that it lacks explicit scriptural evidence. Isaiah 42:21 is the closest that Grotius can find to a supportive text: 'It pleased the Lord for the sake of his righteousness to make his law great and glorious' (NIV). In spite of the lack of strong scriptural support, though, there is something to consider here. As we shall see below, some people object to the picture of a God who demands a penalty and cannot forgive without it. 'If I can forgive someone without the need for retribution, why can God not do the same?' they ask. Grotius is trying to answer that question by demanding no punishment for humankind and no transference of our punishment on to Jesus, but still upholding the moral justice of the universe by seeing Jesus as a substitute for us.

As we seek to share the gospel, the picture presented here is both accessible and challenging. A sympathetic seeker might well understand a message that says, 'Look how much God loved us—Christ took our place on the cross,' rather than the more explicit statement, 'God's holiness demanded that someone pay the penalty for sin, and Christ took the punishment for us.' But for those of other faiths, especially the monotheistic faiths of Islam and Judaism, it offers an engagement with the Trinity that is both necessary and challenging. Without such an engagement, we avoid what lies at the heart of our faith—an understanding of the indivisible triune God effecting our salvation. Mission and theology must never stand too far apart.

4 The atonement as victory over sin and evil

Matthew 20:17–28

Known also as the 'ransom' theory of the atonement, this was the dominant view of the cross in the early centuries of the church, supported by Augustine and others. It is based on the view that Satan has control over humankind. Origen emphasised 1 Corinthians 6:20, 'You were bought with a price,' the implication being that Satan was the one paid. The motif of ransom is made more explicit in Mark 10:45 and Matthew 20:28: 'The Son of Man came not to be served but to serve, and to give his life a ransom for many.' The ransom, it was argued, could not have been paid to God; therefore we were bought from the devil. The focus is on the devil who demands the life of Christ, rather than on God who demands the sacrifice of his Son.

A modification of this view has had something of a resurgence in recent years through the work of Bishop Gustav Aulen from Sweden (1879–1977), whose book *Christus Victor* brought the concept back into vogue. Aulen argued that the cross represented the liberation of humankind: 'The work of Christ is first and foremost a victory over the powers which hold mankind in bondage: sin, death, and the devil.' He sees a ransom not as some kind of business transaction but as the liberation of humanity from enslavement.

This view of the atonement has a strong appeal from a missional perspective, as the idea of being captive to higher forces is intelligible and recognisable. Men and women understand the struggle involved in being slaves to sin. Like Paul, many will be able to say, 'I am of the flesh… I do the very thing I hate' (Romans 7:14–15).

In the history of the Baptist Missionary Society, there is the story of the headhunting Mizo people from north-east India. In the early years of the 20th century there was no fruit for six years of missional endeavour, but, as the workers came to know the Mizo culture better, they put less emphasis on the gospel of forgiveness of sin and more on the gospel of Christ as the conqueror of evil spirits. The Mizo people lived in fear, captive to the forest spirits, so this message delivered them and revivals began.

Today's generations, for all their newfound freedoms, often sense the need to be truly set free. Perhaps here we can find inspiration for such a gospel message.

5 The atonement as compensation to the Father

Romans 3:21–26

The clear distinction in this view of the atonement is that the cross is not directed primarily at humanity, nor does it involve any payment to Satan. It is God-focused and satisfies a principle solely within God himself. Developed most clearly by Anselm (1033–1109), a former Archbishop of Canterbury, it firmly rejects any notion that Satan had rights over God's creation which required God to act.

Anselm, whose thinking was shaped by the feudal environment in which he lived, rather than the Roman legal environment, sees sin as the offensive denial of our rightful duty to honour God. God's nature demands that he must act to preserve his honour and must seek satisfaction for this denial, either from sinners themselves or from another. Even if humanity could offer satisfaction, the highest we could offer would be that which we should have offered in the first place—namely our perfect obedience and respect. To offer compensatory satisfaction, therefore, someone has to offer more than humanity together could put forward. Thus, the incarnation is integral to salvation. God becomes human in and through the sinless Christ, in order to offer more than we ourselves can ever offer.

Anselm's views were developed later, primarily by Protestant reformers, and today this approach is usually named the 'penal substitution' theory. Scripture certainly offers support for this view, with passages such as our reading for today, Romans 3:21–26. Other passages to consult include Isaiah 53:4–6, 10–11; 2 Corinthians 5:21; Galatians 3:10, 13; 1 Peter 2:24 and 1 Peter 3:18.

This persuasive view of the atonement leaves intact the absolute supremacy of God. Even in the rebellions of humanity, the angels and creation itself, nothing stands over God to make demands of him. The demands are internal to God himself, whose love is such that he pays the price for our sinfulness and overthrows the powers that hold his creation in captivity. Contrary to some critiques, in this view the Father is not set against the Son, for the Son's will is entirely at one with the Father's. In missional terms, this is good news of the highest order. The price is paid. Hallelujah!

6 Taking our place at the cross

Matthew 27:41–44

We began the week by reminding ourselves that no theory of the atonement can grasp its fullness. Having surveyed the scene and grasped some of the various theories, we come back to this: we are a people of the cross. The cross should never be an embarrassment to us; it is the scene of the final victory battle.

Consider those in today's passage who mocked and taunted Jesus on the cross. Their basis was this: if he was who he said he was, he could save himself. We may be tempted to say that he chose not to do so, out of love. There is truth in this, but I want to suggest that perhaps his accusers were right: he could not save himself. Even his Father could not save him. At least, he could not be saved and remain true to his own nature.

The Bible makes clear that God is love. His actions must always be true to his essential nature: God can do nothing contrary to love. So perhaps we need to entertain the idea that even from the moment of creation, God saw that his creation would fall into sin and would need to be redeemed. Still, out of love, he created the cosmos and chose a people to be a light to the world. He sent his Son through his chosen people, with Father, Son and Holy Spirit remaining utterly at one in this mission of redemption. Could Jesus have been saved from the cross? No, not if the triune God was to remain consistent to his essential being.

What, then, held Jesus to the cross? Was it God's desire to show the full extent of his love (Day 2)? Well, he certainly did that. Did Jesus die so that the moral order of the universe would be upheld (Day 3)? Maybe he did. In dying, did he liberate us from the powers of evil that cast a shadow over us and so easily destroy us (Day 4)? We can easily argue that. Or did he die not because some external evil power had a hold over us but because God's infinite holiness demanded that death itself, the penalty for all unholiness, had to be destroyed (Day 5)? Scripture speaks clearly on that.

Having surveyed the scene, we stand in awe at the cross. We cannot yet fathom its true depth, but the day is coming when we will.

Guidelines

Here are some ideas to ponder from this week's studies:

- Fr Maximilian Kolbe was a Polish priest who was murdered in a concentration camp, having offered to die in place of another. There is power in a life lived as a wonderful example to others. Consider others known to you who, probably in lesser ways, have lived exemplary lives.
- 'And love is not a victory march; it's a cold and it's a broken "Hallelujah".' Take a quiet moment and consider moments when, in your life, love has hurt. How might this draw us closer to Christ? Has it done so for you?
- We know the reality of doing the very things we hate (Romans 7:14–15). Consider how the image of the cross—its rough nature, with nails driven in hard—might help us consider the battle to quell our sinful nature. Pray about this today.
- Sometimes we drive a wedge between Father and Son, asking, 'Why can't God be as loving and forgiving as we are?' Meditate for a moment on how we can see the cross not as a place of division but as a place of complete and perfect triune togetherness.

1 The promise of the resurrection

John 2:13–25

The resurrection is one of the central features of biblical Christianity, and, as we will see this week, its importance cannot be overstated. The physical resurrection of the body is present even in Old Testament teaching, although it is not a major strand. Commentators are divided on the questions: to what extent are these texts literal or metaphorical, and are they to be personalised or do they somehow refer to Israel? Job voices his hope that 'after my skin has been destroyed, yet in my flesh I will see God' (Job 19:25–26, NIV). Isaiah 26:19 declares to Israel, 'Your dead shall live, their corpses shall rise.' Elsewhere we find references to God reversing death (for example, 1 Kings 17:17–24; Ezekiel 37:12–14) and, in 1 Samuel 2:6, Hannah cites the Lord's ability to raise up those who have died.

Jesus, of course, understood these things deeply. He alluded to his death and resurrection in John 2:19–22 and also spoke of the 'sign of Jonah' (Matthew 12:39; 16:4). After Peter's confession in Caesarea Philippi he began to speak openly about his death, saying that on the third day he would be raised (Matthew 16:21). Very significantly, after his death, his accusers told Pilate to post a guard at the tomb because 'we remember what that imposter said while he was still alive, "After three days I will rise again"' (Matthew 27:62–63).

So the resurrection has history, as we say. It wasn't a story that appeared out of thin air, concocted by Jesus' followers to overcome their despair at his death. But here's the thing: the early disciples' belief in the resurrection was not based on their study of the Old Testament texts or their memory of things Jesus had said. No one was really anticipating the resurrection. Indeed, on the road to Emmaus Jesus chides the two disciples for not understanding what had been taught. No, it was the physical encounter with the risen Jesus that catapulted the church forward with a gospel of resurrection, and it's the physical embodiment of resurrection life that must stand at the heart of the mission of the church. It's not good enough to teach it: we have to live it.

2 The physicality of the resurrection

John 20:1–29

It is deeply important that we understand the resurrection to be a physical rather than mythological or merely theological event.

Compared with the divinity of the triune God, our humanity pales into insignificance. None the less, our humanity is God's creation; it bears the image of the Trinity (Genesis 1:26) and was declared by God to be the pinnacle of his creation. Furthermore, the incarnation of Jesus carries with it the implication that our humanity was capable of bearing the Christ-child, with no suggestion that his humanity detracted from his divinity. On the contrary, the writer to the Hebrews describes the human Jesus as 'the exact imprint of God's very being' (Hebrews 1:3).

When our bodies are described as 'a temple of the Holy Spirit' (1 Corinthians 6:19), we are reminded that our bodies are also capable of bearing God's image, just as Jesus' body did. This has practical implications for holy and healthy living (in matters as basic as food and drink, drugs and exercise) and ethical implications for the protection of life, young or old, able-bodied or disabled.

The roots of Christian service are to be found here also, at least in part. All over the world, in the most remote places, we find Christian hospitals and schools, orphanages and hospices. We see foodbanks and advice centres in our own cities, too. They all flow from our understanding that God views men, women and children as those who bear his image, those he created, those he loves and died to redeem. Such love flows not from our innate goodness but from the God who has made himself known to us in bodily form in Christ, and the Christ who taught us to emulate what he did 'for the least' of his family members (Matthew 25:31–40).

Today's text reminds us that the resurrection was a physical experience, and the mission of the church needs to be tangible too—feeding the hungry, clothing the naked, and giving shelter to the homeless and the refugee. This is the mission of the church. Never, ever let it be thought that caring for the poor or healing the sick is the warm-up act for the 'real' task of evangelism. That would be an insult to the God who created us in his image, who took on our flesh and whose word speaks of a bodily resurrection.

3 The transforming power of resurrection

Luke 24:1–35

When I read the familiar accounts of the post-resurrection appearances of Jesus, I am still struck by the language used to describe the changes that took place in the lives of those involved. The women who went to the tomb were first perplexed (v. 4), then terrified on seeing the angels (v. 5), but they still had the confidence to tell the disciples about it. Although Peter and the others thought the account was 'an idle tale' (v. 11), Peter went to the tomb anyway and then he was amazed (v. 12).

When Mary Magdalene encountered Jesus in the garden, she was distraught, weeping outside the tomb (John 20:11). Minutes later she was scurrying away to proclaim excitedly, 'I have seen the Lord!' (v. 18). That same evening, Jesus appeared to the disciples in a room that was 'locked for fear of the Jews' (v. 19) and within minutes the timid disciples 'rejoiced' (v. 20).

It's the walk to Emmaus, however, that stands out (Luke 24:13–35). Two dejected disciples are walking away from Jerusalem, downcast with shattered hopes. Indeed, so downcast are they that they do not recognise the stranger who joins them, and they chide him for not knowing what has taken place in the city in recent days. They mention that the women 'astounded us' with news that he was alive (vv. 22, 23) but evidently they could not bring themselves to believe it.

The transformation happens over a meal, when bread is taken, blessed, broken and shared. Instantly their lives are changed, they return to the place of apparent defeat, and they too proclaim, 'He is risen.'

So many people today walk that disconsolate path—defeats behind them and no hope before them. The mission of the church is to join the journey, walk alongside, listen, empathise and, in due course, share the good news that Jesus is alive. But that takes time: it needs simple meals and late-night conversations. It needs a familiarity with the scriptures and a degree of patience, for not all will want to hear the first time, if at all. God asks us to be involved in the process. Like the bread used in the meal, God can take us, bless us, break us where necessary, and share us with those along our pathway. Eyes will be opened as the risen Christ is recognised.

4 The significance of the resurrection

1 Corinthians 15:3–19

Writing to the Corinthian church, Paul reminds them of the fundamentals of the gospel, the things that are of 'first importance'—that Christ died, was buried, was raised again, and appeared to the disciples and then to hundreds of others (1 Corinthians 15:3–4). He then stays with the idea of resurrection, driving home the point that if there is no resurrection, then there is no gospel. 'If Christ has not been raised... your faith has been in vain' (v. 14), because 'you are still in your sins' (v. 17) and 'those who have died in Christ have perished' (v. 18).

This could not be more straightforward, but, dare I ask, is it really true? The miraculous birth of Jesus, his life and ministry, miracles and healings, not to mention his sacrificial death—are these not of value too? Are these not of inestimable worth as revelations of God's character and his being? Indeed they are, but two complications arise.

First, there is an issue of truth. If the New Testament witness to Christ's resurrection is not reliable, the whole edifice of truth begins to crumble. Maybe the miracles were embellishments and the healings were overhyped. Maybe Jesus didn't die, after all. Once you remove a central tenet of faith, where does it stop?

Second, there is a fundamental question here about our understanding of reality. The good news of Jesus—his birth, life, death and resurrection—is to be understood in the context of the separation of men and women from God. This separation is the product of sin and is infinite in nature—as far apart as we can conceive holiness and sinfulness to be. Without the death of Jesus, we do not see him as entering into our experience; without the resurrection, his dying is no different from ours. Only the resurrection holds out the hope that our separation will be overcome—in fact, that it has *already* been overcome.

Putting it bluntly, there is no gospel left if Christ has not been raised from the dead. We cannot face a broken, messed-up world and hold on to the hope that all will be well unless Christ went into death, destroyed it and rose to new life. In missional terms, this is one of the hard edges. We can take it or leave it, but we mustn't feel we can tamper with it.

5 The impact of the resurrection

Acts 2:14–32

Name an event that changed the world—vote now! The invention of the wheel, or the printing press, or the worldwide web? All would be worthy candidates, but none has the eternal significance of Christ's resurrection. Our lives are finite, and wheels, books and internet won't make an ounce of difference beyond the day we die—but the resurrection will.

This truth was self-evident to the disciples. Filled with the Holy Spirit (Acts 2:1–13), the fearful, fragile group suddenly had something to live for and, if necessary, die for. Peter emerges as the leader and raises his voice, with the other disciples gathered around him (v. 14). He pleads with the crowds to 'listen to what I say', echoing the prophets of previous generations. Peter builds a bridge to these 'men of Judea', reminding them that their prophet Joel prophesied about a day like this (vv. 16–21). He directs them to Jesus, born among them, a miracle worker who was betrayed, crucified and raised. Here we have the gospel in a nutshell (vv. 22–24), and they witnessed it all (v. 32).

That day, thousands were converted and baptised. Miracles happened (2:43), the poor were helped and the seeds of the church started to grow (vv. 46–47). Throughout the book of Acts we see this growth taking place before our eyes as men and women devote themselves to the mission of the church. Some, like Stephen, gave their lives as martyrs (Acts 7). A woman named Junia, numbered among the apostles, was evidently a leader of the church (Romans 16:7), while Lydia used her financial means to support Paul's ministries (Acts 16:14–15). All of this, and more besides, happened solely because of the cross and resurrection. The enabling power of the Holy Spirit was the catalyst to action, but the core message was the cosmic overthrow of all that passed for bleak normality.

As many in today's world have lost sight of God, so they have also lost sight of life beyond the here-and-now. Many people without faith even see death as good news, an escape from the travails and presumed meaninglessness of life. Such blindness is tragic. Mission that lives and proclaims resurrection is a gospel that will also bring meaning back into daily life. It's not just a hopeful message for tomorrow; it's a message with huge impact for today.

6 Resurrection today

1 Peter 1:1–12

I am surprised by the number of people I meet who have never seen a dead body. A few generations ago, this would have been unthinkable, as it is in many other parts of the world today. So often, our contemporary world takes death out of the picture. We use phrases like 'passed away' rather than 'died', and we hold a 'thanksgiving service', usually without the body in the church, rather than a funeral. There's nothing wrong in these things but they do illustrate the marginalisation of death in society. So, let's get real.

In today's world there is less fear about the process of dying, as pain can usually be controlled. The greater fear concerns the onset of degenerative diseases that can't be cured and affect our quality of life. Then, death can be seen as a welcome relief. As for life after death, some will say, 'That's it—there is no afterlife,' while others voice vague hopes of seeing loved ones again. For billions, especially the poor without access to healthcare and those living in the shadow of war and violence, death is still a menacing presence, something that needs to be transformed by hope. In short, there is still a job to do, a mission to undertake.

In the face of these dark realities, the resurrection brings a radiant burst of light. Death is not the end at all. There is something even more exciting just around the corner, where the brokenness of this life is no more (Revelation 21:3–4). The apostle Peter, in today's passage, speaks of 'a living hope through the resurrection of Jesus Christ' and a glorious inheritance that is 'kept in heaven for you' (1 Peter 1:3–4).

The challenge for us is to live as resurrection people. Look at the television news tonight and consider what the hope of resurrection might mean for the people affected negatively by personal, national or global events. If the best the world can offer is 'Well, one day we'll die and all this agony will be over,' that is where our gospel both offers and demonstrates an alternative. We proclaim resurrection to the poor and the downtrodden, as well as the rich and successful, and by so doing we confront sin and death. Those who have no answer have no mission. The Christian Church has both.

Guidelines

This week we've looked at the resurrection and its central place in our faith.

On Day 3, I suggested that God can use us as he used the bread to open the eyes of those walking to Emmaus. If God is to use you, what might it mean for God to 'take you, bless you, break you and give you'? Pray for the grace to hear God's voice.

A lot of people in today's culture don't understand the message or the mission of the church, so our challenge is both to embody and to interpret it. This act of interpretation is often called the hermeneutic of the gospel. The late Bishop Lesslie Newbigin wrote, 'I am suggesting that the only answer, the only hermeneutic of the gospel, is a congregation of men and women who believe it and live by it' (*The Gospel in a Pluralist Society*, Eerdmans, 1989, p. 227).

At the time of writing, my local church has gone through a catalogue of major illnesses affecting men and women of all ages, primarily with cancer. Our church has coped and cared well. Regularly, people arrive at the church, invited or uninvited, and find a welcome. Often people come to our church or encounter our people in the town and find a listening ear, an encouraging word or a praying companion, if that's what they need. Further afield we see people serving the world in farflung places, connected to us by prayer and sacrificial giving. We are an ordinary church, full of ordinary people, living out the extraordinary truth of resurrection.

You might like to think of the ways your church is making tangible the good news that Jesus is alive. What distinguishes the work of the church from secular work of a similar kind? Can you think of transformational opportunities that form the fabric of your church's work?

FURTHER READING

John Stott, *The Cross of Christ*, IVP, 1986.
Alan Mann, *Atonement for a Sinless Society*, Authentic, 2005.
Scott McKnight, *A Community Called Atonement*, Abingdon Press, 2007.
Frank Morison, *Who Moved the Stone?* Authentic, 2006
N.T. Wright, *Surprised by Hope*, SPCK, 2011.

This page is left blank for your notes.

Size isn't everything

LUCY MOORE

If this were a dodgy news site on the web, I might titivate your interest with a headline something like, 'She opened a book: you'll never BELIEVE what she saw there!' But we were nonetheless all taken aback by what we read in Bob Jackson's book *What Makes Churches Grow? Vision and practice in effective mission.* Bob is a church growth consultant and former Archdeacon of Lichfield and has been an enthusiast for Messy Church for many years. In his book, he describes Messy Church as 'the biggest single churchgoing growth phenomenon in this country since the rise of Sunday schools and Methodism at the end of the eighteenth century'.

It's an incredible claim, isn't it? I'm so glad it isn't ours. It raises some interesting questions, such as, what does this growth mean for BRF and what does it mean for churches?

We must reach a tipping point sometime. Nothing can or should keep on growing or it will collapse under its own weight, but at the moment we keep on seeing numerical growth. As you probably know, we invite churches to register their Messy Church on the Directory on www.messychurch.org.uk. This is mostly so that families can find their nearest Messy Church easily; it's also so that we can share resources and news with the leaders, and it also helps us when bishops ask, 'Just how many Messy Churches are there?' You can see exactly how many have registered by looking at the homepage of the website, where the number is automatically updated. (As I glance now, #3240 has been started in Eaglesham in East Kilbride. Hooray!)

I'm conscious, as I write, that even if this article were to be published next week, this figure would already be out of date. By the time you read this, I wonder what number and which exotic location will be on the homepage. The speed of growth and change at the moment is phenomenal. We must try not to take it for granted, but to keep on thanking God for it.

Growth happens on different levels. Numerical growth is exciting, but look at the last throwaway comment in Rachel Hill-Brown's recent email:

I wanted to tell you about our Easter Messy Church. We meet monthly on the second Sunday at 3.30 pm usually and get about 180 people coming... This month we did an extra Messy Church on Maundy Thursday at 10.00 am (first day of school holidays). I had no idea how many to expect but anticipated lower numbers—we had to close the doors when we hit 250 and turned about 30 people away! That felt awful but we were simply full to bursting and any more bodies would have made it unsafe. There were tears! Thankfully we had some balloons to give away, which helped to soften the blow... It was an incredible opportunity to share the Easter story with a whole load of people we don't usually see as well as some regulars. (Oh, and we have more baptism requests too!)

The growth is encouraging and affirming for us as an organisation. The fact that God chose BRF out of all the mission agencies and ministry groups to be the home for Messy Church is something we relish, across all the BRF teams, in and out of the office. The prayers of so many faithful people over so many years since 1922, when BRF began, have made it a fertile vegetable patch for this particular seed to fall into. We feel very blessed to have been given the privilege of nurturing this little sprout as God makes it grow. It's fantastic to be able to create top-quality books and websites and to run social media accounts through the skills of the wider BRF team.

The growth has given us friends and contacts across the world. As Messy Church has popped up in more than 30 countries, as diverse as Canada and Slovenia, New Zealand and Switzerland, we have chatted on Skype, emailed, and welcomed to our homes and to BRF people from many of those countries. We won't forget giggling with the Icelandic pair, or sharing cake with the women from Holland, or advising the pastor from Norway that it might take a little longer than 30 minutes to get from Hampshire to Heathrow on the M3. And on trips overseas, I have met so many ex-pats who say, 'I've read BRF daily notes for the last 50 years and I've been praying for you ever since you joined BRF.' The spread of Messy Church has meant a reinforcement of BRF links across the globe and a deep sense of joy in those friendships. Bjarne Gertz Olsen emailed only today from Denmark: 'Thank you for your Newsletters as I receive. It's so nice to read about what happen in the Messy Church movement. It's really a blessing. And so great to see how Messy Church now is an International movement. It's great.'

However, it becomes increasingly difficult to support the growing network properly. We only have one Jane Leadbetter to support the 95 Regional Coordinators. If Jane was slapdash, this might be OK, but she sees it as her responsibility to pray for them, pastor them (albeit at a distance) and be there for them, for any and every Messy query or moment of triumph. And 95 people need a great deal of support.

Martyn Payne visits Messy Churches to encourage, learn from and advise them, and to highlight to us what issues are being raised across the country. With the best will in the world, Martyn can only take so many fish fingers a week. Most Messy Churches have to be left to get on with it on their own without personal input from BRF.

I try to make sure church gatekeepers like bishops or District Chairs are happy with what's going on in Messy Churches in their denominations, but time is limited and there are (joyfully!) so many denominations involved: how do we listen to the needs and concerns of all 20-plus?

So growth brings joys but also issues for BRF. How do we ensure that Messy Churches are effectively supported without expanding the BRF Messy team into an unwieldy crowd, needing even more admin and structures to make it work, and for which we don't have funding in any case? How do we ensure that we are the wise accompaniers of Messy leaders, not corks in the bottle through lack of resources?

On a bigger scale, what are the denominations going to do about this growth phenomenon in their midst? Will the impressive stats mean that clergy training is altered to help church leaders make the most of the opportunities in the Messy Churches for which they are responsible? Will they help BRF with the constant need for core funding? Will they draw Messy Church strategically into their growth plans? Will they affirm the ministry of lay leaders within the churches? Will they listen to what this rather scruffy angel is saying to the churches about what families this century need from their local church? Or will they politely ignore it and wait for it to go away?

'I planted the seed, Apollos watered it, but God has been making it grow' (1 Corinthians 3:6). If this is God's hand at work, we can only trust that God will grow this strange and messy family in the way that he knows is best.

Lucy Moore is the founder and team leader of BRF's Messy Church.

Guidelines forthcoming issue

DAVID SPRIGGS

The forthcoming issue of *Guidelines* is not to be missed. We are fortunate to have the insights of several writers who are becoming well-established favourites.

Antony Billington, who is the resident Theologian for the London Institute of Contemporary Christianity, shares his reflections on the contribution that the Bible makes to our understanding of our role as Christians in the workplace. Bill Goodman brings the insights he gained through his PhD research, engaging with the Song of Solomon in comparison with contemporary lyrics, all of which comment on the beauty and challenges of the intimate love between a man and a woman. David Kerrigan concludes his series helping us to grasp more clearly the missiological significance of the key phases of the life of Jesus, exploring the way the Holy Spirit deepens the challenge of mission for us in the 21st century.

Of particular note, though, is the number of new contributors who have agreed to write for us. Kate Bruce works as a theologian in Durham, with a special interest on the way we communicate God's truth in our culture. Her notes look at the many ways in which God communicates in the Bible. John Leach brings his varied life experience to bear on the challenges to discipleship today. John is now responsible for encouraging discipleship in the Diocese of Lincoln. Keith Neville adds his grasp of mission in John's Gospel, seeing this as a thread running through the Gospel, not something confined to the well-known 'Paraclete' passages. Another new author for us is Meg Warner, who helps us appreciate the many ways in which the Genesis account of Abraham's life has spoken to God's people.

Continuing the Old Testament theme, Maggie Guite expounds the messages of the 'minor prophets' Joel and Haggai. She brings both scholarship and pastoral sensitivity to the task. In similar vein, I will be unpacking the importance of the book of Amos, focusing on the substantial contribution he makes to our understanding of social justice.

Ultimately all our endeavours to understand the reality of the scriptures are focused on our understanding of and faith in Jesus Christ. Matthew's Gospel, in its own way, is also seeking to relate the Old Testament to the new reality of Jesus the Messiah. So have I left the best till last? Nigel Wright makes another incisive contribution to Guidelines as he continues his insights on Matthew's Gospel, this time taking chapters 19—23. He writes:

A one-dimensional view of Jesus is not possible once we have encountered him in a diversity of settings and encounters.... Everything that comes to us from him, whether in word or deed, needs to be taken extremely seriously if we are to be true to him.

I hope, by now, you can't wait to get your hands on the forthcoming issue of *Guidelines*!

Author profile: Dr Nigel G. Wright

Growing up, I was entirely ignorant of the Bible. My family had lapsed from the faith and the Bible did not figure in our home other than as a place to record genealogy. When I encountered the living Christ for myself at the age of 15, things began to change.

In the small youth group of the church where I was converted, there was a girl I rather fancied, and she knew a lot more than I did. I determined to increase my knowledge! I started with the Gospels and from there worked my way backwards and forwards to pick up the overall picture. This worked well enough, and improved greatly when I switched from the King James Bible to the RSV.

While pursuing modern languages at university, my studies became more serious with the use of an aid entitled *Search the Scriptures*, and intensified considerably while studying for a semester in Salzburg, with time to read and think. It was also during this time that a call to ministry crystallised for me, not least because of the listening to the Bible that I was doing.

Covering the whole Bible and using incisive questions for each passage, *Search the Scriptures* encouraged readers to engage with passages at a more demanding level, thinking through their meaning and implications. When I went on to study theology and prepare for ministry, the demanding study continued, but this time with the advantage of reading the text in the original languages (when I chose to). All of this was highly formative. When it developed into regular teaching and preaching, I was entering decisively into the 'strange world of the Bible'.

It goes without saying that I found the Bible enriching and enlightening. It became the word of God to me. This is not to say that it is unproblematic: it can inspire and infuriate in equal measure. With parts of it, I have yet to understand why they are there and what they have to say. I have learnt that many of us use the Bible to bolster opinions that we already hold, rather than hearing what is actually there. Letting the text speak for itself is a great challenge, particularly when we fear that we might not like what it says. We may have strong views about the primacy of the Bible's authority, but we do like to make sure it conforms to the traditions in which we are comfortable!

Over a lifetime (I am now retired, though not from engaging with scripture), it has become more and more clear to me that the Bible is not, as is often claimed, a book of 'timeless truth'. Quite the opposite: it preserves words that were spoken in very specific contexts, many of which we are unable to reconstruct with certainty; often those same words have been reapplied to later contexts in a cumulative process of events and interpretation. Bible reading should therefore be contextual, seeking to discover what situations were being addressed originally. We need to 'indwell' the text; only then can we begin to discern what these texts might say to contemporary realities. If I have learnt anything, it is that I must not make the Bible into what I would like it to be, but should let it be itself, in all its angularity and distinctiveness. Then I can decide what to do about it.

I have written a number of books, and people who know me sometimes say that, as they read them, they can almost hear me speaking. The point of having written scriptures is that, as we study them, we enter into the mind of the God who has inspired them and who illuminates us by the Spirit as we read. In the words, we hear the Word that is Christ himself. As the Gospel says, they are written 'that you may believe that Jesus is the Christ, the Son of God, and that believing you may have life in his name' (John 20:21, RSV). It works for me.

Dr Nigel G. Wright, Principal Emeritus, Spurgeon's College London

Recommended reading

BRF's 2017 Lent book is by **Amy Boucher Pye**, who will be familiar to readers of *New Daylight* and *Day by Day with God* notes. Moving from Ash Wednesday to Easter Day, daily reflections and prayers help us to experience the living power of the cross of Christ through biblical and modern-day stories of wrongdoing and forgiveness. The following extract is the introduction to the first week of readings, on the Israelite founders of our faith.

In our journey of exploring the living cross as the source of forgiveness and new life, we start on Ash Wednesday at the very beginning, when it all goes wrong as Adam and Eve turn from God. From the start, we see our need for a Saviour, for Jesus to become the new Adam who leads us into life eternal.

We move next to sibling relationships and sibling rivalry, a tearing-apart between brothers that unfortunately continues through the generations, reflecting our need for Jesus' work on the cross. Then we come to our first fallen-but-redeemed founders of the faith, Abram and Sarai, who act on their fears through deception (Abram) and by turning to their own ways of making things happen (Sarai) instead of trusting God. Yet the Lord saves them and fulfils his promises, just as he made good on saving us from the curse of the law.

We encounter more sibling strife with Jacob and Esau, including parents who favour one child over the other and the destruction that follows. And yet God's redemptive work in Jacob brings harmony and reconciliation, hinting at the restored relationships we enjoy at the foot of the cross. Yet more unhappy families greet us in the stories of Joseph and his brothers, but we see also how God redeems the sin and deceit, as Joseph saves his family and God's people from destruction through famine. So too does Jesus save us.

Our extended week ends with Moses, another great leader of God's people. He is a murderer, yet is used by God as his instrument to lead his people to the promised land. We, like Moses, are made new at the living cross, where we can leave behind the old self as we put on the clothes of the new.

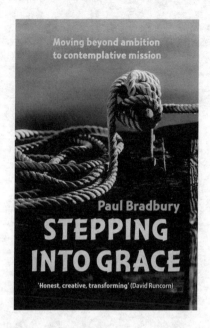

Stepping into Grace finds powerful connections between the call and mission of Jonah and the mission context of our own time. Using the narrative thread of the biblical story to explore ambition, vocation, spirituality, mission, leadership and personal growth, it argues for a ministry rooted in grace, where who we are becoming in Christ provides a foundation for our participation in the mission of God.

Stepping into Grace
Moving beyond ambition to contemplative mission
Paul Bradbury
978 0 85746 523 8 £7.99
brf.org.uk

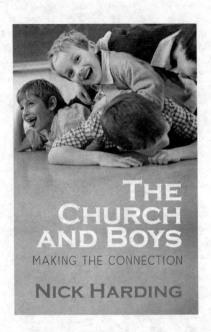

THE
CHURCH
AND BOYS
MAKING THE CONNECTION

NICK HARDING

Why are boys so under-represented in churches? Why do churches find it so difficult to cater for boys? What would help boys in church grow into mature men of faith? This uniquely inspiring book spells out the problem and encourages churches to see it in missional terms. The book includes resources, suggestions and ideas to help boys connect better with the church, with the Bible, and with the Christian faith.

The Church and Boys
Making the connection
Nick Harding
978 0 85746 509 2 £8.99
brf.org.uk

To order

Online: **brfonline.org.uk**
Telephone: +44 (0)1865 319700
Mon–Fri 9.15–17.30

Delivery times within the UK are normally
15 working days. Prices are correct at the time of
going to press but may change without prior notice.

Title	Price	Qty	Total
The Living Cross	£8.99		
Spiritual Growth in a Time of Change	£7.99		
Stepping into Grace	£7.99		
The Church and Boys	£8.99		

POSTAGE AND PACKING CHARGES			
Order value	UK	Europe	Rest of world
Under £7.00	£1.25	£3.00	£5.50
£7.00–£29.99	£2.25	£5.50	£10.00
£30.00 and over	FREE	Prices on request	

Total value of books	
Postage and packing	
Total for this order	

Please complete in BLOCK CAPITALS

Title .... First name/initials .... Surname ....

Address ....

.... Postcode ....

Acc. No. .... Telephone ....

Email ....

Please keep me informed about BRF's books and resources ❑ by email ❑ by post
Please keep me informed about the wider work of BRF ❑ by email ❑ by post

Method of payment

❑ Cheque (made payable to BRF) ❑ MasterCard / Visa

Card no. ☐☐☐☐ ☐☐☐☐ ☐☐☐☐ ☐☐☐☐ ☐☐☐☐ ☐☐☐☐

Valid from ☐☐/☐☐ Expires ☐☐/☐☐ Security code* ☐☐☐
Last 3 digits on the reverse of the card

Signature* .... Date .... /......... /.........
*ESSENTIAL IN ORDER TO PROCESS YOUR ORDER

Please return this form to: BRF, 15 The Chambers, Vineyard, Abingdon OX14 3FE | enquiries@brf.org.uk
To read our terms and find out about cancelling your order, please visit **brfonline.org.uk/terms**

How to encourage Bible reading in your church

BRF has been helping individuals connect with the Bible for over 90 years. We want to support churches as they seek to encourage church members into regular Bible reading.

Order a Bible reading resources pack

This pack is designed to give your church the tools to publicise our Bible reading notes. It includes:

• Sample Bible reading notes for your congregation to try.

• Publicity resources, including a poster.

• A church magazine feature about Bible reading notes.

The pack is free, but we welcome a £5 donation to cover the cost of postage. If you require a pack to be sent outside the UK or require a specific number of sample Bible reading notes, please contact us for postage costs. More information about what the current pack contains is available on our website.

How to order and find out more

• Visit biblereadingnotes.org.uk/for-churches

• Telephone BRF on +44 (0)1865 319700 Mon–Fri 9.15–17.30

• Write to us at BRF, 15 The Chambers, Vineyard, Abingdon OX14 3FE

Keep informed about our latest initiatives

We are continuing to develop resources to help churches encourage people into regular Bible reading, wherever they are on their journey. Join our email list at biblereadingnotes.org.uk/helpingchurches to stay informed about the latest initiatives that your church could benefit from.

Introduce a friend to our notes

We can send information about our notes and current prices for you to pass on. Please contact us.

BRF Transforming Lives and Communities

BRF is a charity that is passionate about making a difference through the Christian faith. We want to see lives and communities transformed through our creative programmes and resources for individuals, churches and schools. We are doing this by resourcing:

- **Christian growth and understanding of the Bible.** Through our Bible reading notes, books, digital resources, Quiet Days and other events, we're resourcing individuals, groups and leaders in churches for their own spiritual journey and for their ministry.

- **Church outreach in the local community.** BRF is the home of three programmes that churches are embracing to great effect as they seek to engage with their local communities: Messy Church, Who Let The Dads Out? and The Gift of Years.

- **Teaching Christianity in primary schools.** Our Barnabas in Schools team is working with primary-aged children and their teachers, enabling them to explore Christianity creatively within the school curriculum.

- **Children's and family ministry.** Through our Barnabas in Churches and Faith in Homes websites and published resources, we're working with churches and families, enabling children under 11, and the adults working with them, to explore Christianity creatively and bring the Bible alive.

Do you share our vision?

Sales of our books and Bible reading notes cover the cost of producing them. However, our other programmes are funded primarily by donations, grants and legacies. If you share our vision, would you help us to transform even more lives and communities? Your prayers and financial support are vital for the work that we do.

- You could support BRF's ministry with a one-off gift or regular donation (using the response form on page 153).

- You could consider making a bequest to BRF in your will (page 152).

- You could encourage your church to support BRF as part of your church's giving to home mission—perhaps focusing on a specific area of our ministry, or a particular member of our Barnabas team.

- Most important of all, you could support BRF with your prayers.

Make a lasting difference through a gift in your will

BRF's story began almost a century ago when a vicar in Brixton, south London, introduced daily Bible readings to help his congregation 'get a move on spiritually'. Today our creative programmes and resources impact thousands of lives and communities across the UK and worldwide, from Brixton to Brisbane.

One such programme is **Who Let The Dads Out?**, which is working to transform family relationships in the UK by turning the hearts of fathers to their children and the hearts of children to their fathers (Malachi 4:6). The relationship between father and child is spiritually significant, and when you lead a father from a non-Christian family to Christ there is a 93 per cent probability that the family will follow. Who Let The Dads Out? is making ready a people prepared for the Lord and causing a cultural shift, encouraging churches to value and invest in ministry to fathers.

If you share our passion for making a difference through the Christian faith, please consider leaving a gift in your will to BRF. Gifts in wills are an important source of income for us and they don't need to be huge to make a real difference. For every £1 you give, we will invest 88p back into charitable activities. Just imagine what we could do over the next century with your help.

For further information about making a gift to BRF in your will, please visit brf.org.uk or contact Sophie on 01865 319700 or email giving@brf.org.uk.

Whatever you can do or give, we thank you for your support.

SHARING OUR VISION – MAKING A GIFT

I would like to make a gift to support BRF. Please use my gift for:

☐ where it is needed most ☐ Barnabas Children's Ministry

☐ Messy Church ☐ Who Let The Dads Out? ☐ The Gift of Years

Title	First name/initials	Surname

Address

	Postcode

Email

Telephone

Signature	Date

giftaid it You can add an extra 25p to every £1 you give.

Please treat as Gift Aid donations all qualifying gifts of money made

☐ today, ☐ in the past four years, ☐ and in the future.

I am a UK taxpayer and understand that if I pay less Income Tax and/or Capital Gains Tax in the current tax year than the amount of Gift Aid claimed on all my donations, it is my responsibility to pay any difference.

☐ My donation does not qualify for Gift Aid.

Please notify BRF if you want to cancel this Gift Aid declaration, change your name or home address, or no longer pay sufficient tax on your income and/or capital gains.

Please complete other side of form ➲

Please return this form to:
BRF, 15 The Chambers, Vineyard, Abingdon OX14 3FE

The Bible Reading Fellowship is a Registered Charity (233280)

SHARING OUR VISION – MAKING A GIFT

Regular giving

By Direct Debit:

☐ I would like to make a regular gift of £ [____] per month/quarter/year.
Please also complete the Direct Debit instruction on page 159.

By Standing Order:

Please contact Priscilla Kew, tel. +44 (0)1235 462305; giving@brf.org.uk

One-off donation

Please accept my gift of:

☐ £10 ☐ £50 ☐ £100 Other £ [____]

by (delete as appropriate):

☐ Cheque/Charity Voucher payable to 'BRF'

☐ MasterCard/Visa/Debit card/Charity card

Name on card

Card no. [_][_][_][_] [_][_][_][_] [_][_][_][_] [_][_][_][_]

Valid from [M][M][Y][Y] Expires [M][M][Y][Y]

Security code* [_][_][_] *Last 3 digits on the reverse of the card
ESSENTIAL IN ORDER TO PROCESS YOUR PAYMENT

Signature   Date

We like to acknowledge all donations. However, if you do not wish to
receive an acknowledgement, please tick here ☐

← Please complete other side of form

Please return this form to:
BRF, 15 The Chambers, Vineyard, Abingdon OX14 3FE

BRF

The Bible Reading Fellowship is a Registered Charity (233280)

GUIDELINES SUBSCRIPTION RATES

Please note our new subscription rates for the coming year. From the May 2017 issue, the new subscription rates will be:

Individual subscriptions
covering 3 issues for under 5 copies, payable in advance
(including postage & packing):

	UK	Europe	Rest of world
Guidelines	£16.50	£24.60	£28.50
Guidelines 3-year subscription (9 issues)	£45.00	N/A	N/A

Group subscriptions
covering 3 issues for 5 copies or more, sent to **one** UK address (post free):

Guidelines	£13.20 per set of 3 issues p.a.

Please note that the annual billing period for group subscriptions runs from 1 May to 30 April.

Overseas group subscription rates
Available on request. Please email enquiries@brf.org.uk.

Copies may also be obtained from Christian bookshops:

Guidelines	£4.40 per copy

All our Bible reading notes can be ordered online by visiting
biblereadingnotes.org.uk/subscriptions

For information about our other Bible reading notes,
and apps for iPhone and iPod touch, visit
biblereadingnotes.org.uk

GUIDELINES INDIVIDUAL SUBSCRIPTION FORM

All our Bible reading notes can be ordered online by visiting
biblereadingnotes.org.uk/subscriptions

☐ I would like to take out a subscription:

Title .... First name/initials .... Surname ....

Address ....

.... Postcode ....

Telephone .... Email ....

Please send *Guidelines* beginning with the May 2017 / September 2017 / January 2018 issue (*delete as appropriate*):

(*please tick box*)

	UK	Europe	Rest of world
Guidelines	☐ £16.50	☐ £24.60	☐ £28.50
Guidelines 3-year subscription	☐ £45.00	N/A	N/A

Total enclosed £ _____ (cheques should be made payable to 'BRF')

Please charge my MasterCard / Visa ☐ Debit card ☐ with £ _____

Card no. ☐☐☐☐ ☐☐☐☐ ☐☐☐☐ ☐☐☐☐

Valid from ☐☐/☐☐ Expires ☐☐/☐☐ Security code* ☐☐☐

Last 3 digits on the reverse of the card

Signature* .... Date ..../......./.......

*ESSENTIAL IN ORDER TO PROCESS YOUR PAYMENT

To set up a Direct Debit, please also complete the Direct Debit instruction on page 159 and return it to BRF with this form.

Please return this form with the appropriate payment to:
BRF, 15 The Chambers, Vineyard, Abingdon OX14 3FE

To read our terms and find out about cancelling your order, please visit **brfonline.org.uk/terms**.

The Bible Reading Fellowship (BRF) is a Registered Charity (233280)

GL0117

GUIDELINES GIFT SUBSCRIPTION FORM

☐ I would like to give a gift subscription (please provide both names and addresses):

Title .... First name/initials .... Surname ....

Address ....

.... Postcode ....

Telephone .... Email ....

Gift subscription name ....

Gift subscription address ....

.... Postcode ....

Gift message (20 words max. or include your own gift card):

....

....

Please send *Guidelines* beginning with the May 2017 / September 2017 / January 2018 issue (*delete as appropriate*):

(please tick box)	UK	Europe	Rest of world
Guidelines	☐ £16.50	☐ £24.60	☐ £28.50
Guidelines 3-year subscription	☐ £45.00	N/A	N/A

Total enclosed £ .... (cheques should be made payable to 'BRF')

Please charge my MasterCard / Visa ☐ Debit card ☐ with £ ....

Card no. ☐☐☐☐ ☐☐☐☐ ☐☐☐☐ ☐☐☐☐

Valid from ☐☐☐☐ Expires ☐☐☐☐ Security code* ☐☐☐

Last 3 digits on the reverse of the card

Signature* .... Date ....../....../......

*ESSENTIAL IN ORDER TO PROCESS YOUR PAYMENT

To set up a Direct Debit, please also complete the Direct Debit instruction on page 159 and return it to BRF with this form.

Please return this form with the appropriate payment to:
BRF, 15 The Chambers, Vineyard, Abingdon OX14 3FE

To read our terms and find out about cancelling your order, please visit **brfonline.org.uk/terms**.

The Bible Reading Fellowship (BRF) is a Registered Charity (233280)

DIRECT DEBIT PAYMENT

You can pay for your annual subscription to our Bible reading notes using Direct Debit. You need only give your bank details once, and the payment is made automatically every year until you cancel it. If you would like to pay by Direct Debit, please use the form opposite, entering your BRF account number under 'Reference number'.

You are fully covered by the Direct Debit Guarantee:

The Direct Debit Guarantee

- This Guarantee is offered by all banks and building societies that accept instructions to pay Direct Debits.

- If there are any changes to the amount, date or frequency of your Direct Debit, The Bible Reading Fellowship will notify you 10 working days in advance of your account being debited or as otherwise agreed. If you request The Bible Reading Fellowship to collect a payment, confirmation of the amount and date will be given to you at the time of the request.

- If an error is made in the payment of your Direct Debit, by The Bible Reading Fellowship or your bank or building society, you are entitled to a full and immediate refund of the amount paid from your bank or building society.

- If you receive a refund you are not entitled to, you must pay it back when The Bible Reading Fellowship asks you to.

- You can cancel a Direct Debit at any time by simply contacting your bank or building society. Written confirmation may be required. Please also notify us.

GL0117

The Bible Reading Fellowship

Instruction to your bank or building society to pay by Direct Debit

Please fill in the whole form using a ballpoint pen and return it to:
BRF, 15 The Chambers, Vineyard, Abingdon OX14 3FE

Service User Number: | 5 | 5 | 8 | 2 | 2 | 9 |

Name and full postal address of your bank or building society

To: The Manager	Bank/Building Society
Address	
	Postcode

Name(s) of account holder(s)

Branch sort code

| | | | – | | | – | | | |

Bank/Building Society account number

Reference number

Instruction to your Bank/Building Society

Please pay The Bible Reading Fellowship Direct Debits from the account detailed
in this instruction, subject to the safeguards assured by the Direct Debit Guarantee.
I understand that this instruction may remain with The Bible Reading Fellowship
and, if so, details will be passed electronically to my bank/building society.

Signature(s)

Banks and Building Societies may not accept Direct Debit instructions for some types
of account.

This page is left blank for your notes.